INSTANT

AMERICAN
LITERATURE

INSTANT

AMERICAN LITERATURE

BY LAURIE ROZAKIS, PH.D.

A Byron Preiss Book

FAWCETT·COLUMBINE • NEW YORK

Copyright © 1995 by Byron Preiss Visual Publications, Inc.

Cartoon Credits: Copyright © 1994 Aaron Bacall–85, 148, 187.
© 1994 Roz Chast–166. © 1994 Boris Drucker–161. © 1994 Ed Frascino–48.
© 1994 Mort Gerberg–83, 91, 206. © 1994 Liz Haberfeld–74.
© 1994 Tim Haggerty–156. © 1994 John Jonik–137.
© 1994 John O'Brien–204.

The Cartoon Bank, Inc., located in Yonkers, NY, is a computerized archive featuring the work of over fifty of the country's top cartoonists.

Illustration credits: © 1995 Archive Holdings 2, 5, 6, 8, 20, 23, 25, 34, 40, 42, 43, 44, 49, 53, 54, 58, 61, 62, 64, 66, 70, 78, 82, 83, 86, 89, 93, 95, 98, 101, 107, 108, 116, 121, 122, 125, 126, 130, 136, 142, 146, 150, 153, 169, 177, 181, 189, 192, 195, 196, 206, 212, 215, 222, 223, 228. © Amherst College Library–172.

Library of Congress Catalog Card Number: 94-90821

ISBN: 449-90700-7

Cover design by Heidi North

Manufactured in the United States of America

First Edition: August 1995

10 9 8 7 6 5 4 3 2 1

To The Man—
for too many reasons to list

CONTENTS

INTRODUCTION   ix

CHAPTER 1
Washington Irving: *The Sketch Book*   3

CHAPTER 2
James Fenimore Cooper: *The Leatherstocking Tales*   21

CHAPTER 3
The Transcendentalists
(Ralph Waldo Emerson and
Henry David Thoreau):
Nature and *Walden*   41

CHAPTER 4
Nathaniel Hawthorne: *The Scarlet Letter*   59

CHAPTER 5
Edgar Allan Poe: "The Raven"   79

CHAPTER 6
Harriet Beecher Stowe: *Uncle Tom's Cabin*   99

CHAPTER 7
Frederick Douglass: *Narrative of the
Life of Frederick Douglass, an American Slave*   117

CHAPTER 8
Walt Whitman: *Leaves of Grass*   **131**

CHAPTER 9
Herman Melville: *Moby Dick*   **151**

CHAPTER 10
Emily Dickinson: " 'Hope' is the
thing with feathers"   **173**

CHAPTER 11
Mark Twain: *Huckleberry Finn*   **193**

CHAPTER 12
Stephen Crane: *The Red Badge of Courage*   **213**

INDEX   **231**

INTRODUCTION

It's Friday night and you're in the mood for a *real* book. Your soul is crying out for a novel with *meaning*. You've read too many horror novels lately—books where a bloodthirsty psychopath stalks a beautiful coed who just happens to be the love interest of a hardboiled ex-cop with a soft spot for women in distress. It's time for a book with some character development.

So you head down to the local bookstore and scan the literature section. What should you buy? To make sure you cover all the bases, you pick out an armload of titles you dimly recall from American Literature 101. Two months later the books remain where you left them, unread. The dust on the stack is pretty impressive. Time passes. A lot of time. You know it's all over when you find yourself unplugging your phone for the George Romero film festival. You feel cheap in the morning.

Or maybe the date of your dreams believes his life changed when he read *Leaves of Grass*—and so, to align yourself fully with this dreamboat's innermost heart, you'll have to sponge up the works of Walt Whitman. You *could* spend weeks in a library picking up an intimate knowledge of the poet's work. *Or* you could spend *more* time with the love o' your life by picking up *Instant American Literature*.

We Can Tell: *Instant American Literature* Is for You

In this survey of the best writing of nineteenth-century America, you'll learn how the works of thirteen famous authors fit into literary history's big picture. You'll get a list of each author's best-known works, a concise biography, and a critical analysis revealing the literary trends these writers established—or ignored. In addition, a variety of lighthearted sidebars will balance weightier topics like theme, character, plot, and context. You will come away with a handle on the hidden allusions and unexpected connections that make great literature . . . great.

American Literature in the Nineteenth Century

In the early nineteenth century, readers on this side of the pond hungered for what might be called a "national literature." This meant writing that relied on uniquely American themes, avoiding the slavish imitation of European styles that had previously guided the world of American letters. Two New Yorkers—Washington Irving and James Fenimore Cooper—were among the earliest homegrown wordsmiths of note. Both men were deeply affected by Romanticism, a literary and artistic movement that began in eighteenth-century Europe. The hallmarks of Romanticism were an emphasis on emotion, imagination, and the senses; an interest in the plight of the average man; an exaltation of nature; and a bias toward melancholy. Each author adapted the habits of Romantic literature to the unique circumstances of his newly born frontier nation. Irving's "Legend of Sleepy Hollow" sparked an interest in writing that contained what we now call "local color." Cooper's *Last of the Mohicans* created a mythology of his own. He focused on the tragedy inherent in the subjugation of the Native Americans, and in so doing made his work a philosophical quest for the meaning of the frontier.

Irving and Cooper lived in New York and so made that state the nation's first literary capital, but in truth writers flourished all across America. The South produced the lugubrious writing of Edgar Allan Poe. Poe's poetry was originally influenced by the Romantic poetry of Byron and Shelley. However, he is now recognized more for helping to establish the craft and conventions of short story writing and for introducing such popular subgenres as the detective story and the tale of horror.

The literary movement known as Transcendentalism began in Boston, Massachusetts, a city that had acquired a tradition of learning through the presence of Harvard College, as well as through the New England clergy's reputation for scholarship. Transcendentalists were philosophical idealists who believed that the human mind was the ultimate source of human knowledge and that each person must be true to his or her own unique inspiration. The Transcendental mood was best expressed by the writings of Ralph Waldo Emerson and Henry David Thoreau. Their works celebrated the divinity of the individual, the sanctity of nature, and the primacy of intuition over reason. Thoreau's *Walden* was a layman's guide for living an honorable, wholesome life. Emerson defined American poetry. His verse, celebrating ordinary experience rather than epic themes, was more concerned with fact than eloquence.

The Transcendentalists were also deeply concerned about conventional Christianity and death. Emily Dickinson, who lived in Amherst, Massachusetts, wrote poetry that dealt with the themes of death and immortality and the desire to know the purpose of life. Her rich visual imagery, unique style, and unusual metaphors paved the way for modern poetry.

Nathaniel Hawthorne was also part of the Transcendental crowd in Massachusetts. However, due to his fixation with America's Puritan past, he rejected the idealistic teaching of the movement. His "allegories of the heart" such as *The Scarlet Letter* raised guilt and sin to an art form, and his keen psychological insights prepared American readers for the works of Herman Melville.

Melville began his writing career after seven years at sea. *Moby Dick* is ostensibly a sea adventure. Beneath the superficial action of the book, however, one finds a dark and complex story of human obsession. The tale can be read as an allegory of the risks required to bend nature to the will of humanity. Though Melville wrote what can be considered one of America's greatest novels, *Moby Dick* was unappreciated by the general public during his life and he died in relative obscurity.

Like Melville, Walt Whitman was not fully appreciated until this century. Whitman wrote only one book—*Leaves of Grass*—but published nine different versions, the last of which contained 389 poems. His boastful individualism in such poems as "Song of Myself" reveals the freewheeling spirit that has come to typify the American character. Whitman was a champion of "free verse" and achieved recognition as the poet who had given his country a lyrical voice of its own.

Frederick Douglass's *Narrative of the Life of Frederick Douglass, an American Slave* is a story of self-emancipation. Douglass was a runaway slave who risked recapture to tell his story and to speak out against slavery. More than an autobiography, his story is an allegory that shows how slavery corrupts the human spirit and robs both master and slave of their freedom. Douglass became one of the boldest, most resolute enemies of racial injustice.

Another writer who spoke out against slavery was Harriet Beecher Stowe. Legend has it that when President Lincoln met Stowe during the Civil War, he remarked, "So this is the little lady who wrote the book that caused the big war!" He was referring to Stowe's *Uncle Tom's Cabin*, which aroused such strong sympathy for slaves that it heightened the division between proslavery and antislavery factions and caused seismic shifts in America's attitudes toward the South's "peculiar institution."

The strong feelings aroused by slavery were also put to use by Mark Twain (the pen name of Samuel Langhorne Clemens) in *The Adventures of Huckleberry Finn*. Twain's mythic tale of death, rebirth, freedom, and human bondage uses the metaphor of slavery as an emblem for the universal themes of institutionalized injustice and social bondage. Besides achieving these lofty aims, however, Twain also succeeded in capturing the diverse dialects of American English. He unerringly captured the rhythms, vocabulary, and tone of regional speech to create characters who are as lifelike today as they were a hundred years ago.

Unlike the humorous narrative that characterized Twain's style, Naturalist authors such as Stephen Crane examined a darker side of American life. The characters in their novels were mere puppets in the grip of forces beyond their control. One such story was Stephen Crane's *Maggie: A Girl of the Streets.* This tale of a young woman destroyed by her squalid environment was so bleak that publishers were afraid to release it to the public. After this grim tale, Crane wrote *The Red Badge of Courage.* This story of courage and cowardice in battle is considered the first modern war novel, and over a century later it has become like the vast majority of the books covered in *Instant American Literature,* a must for all students of the American literary tradition.

INSTANT

AMERICAN
LITERATURE

Washington Irving, the Father of American Literature

CHAPTER 1

WASHINGTON IRVING
(1783–1859)

YOU MUST REMEMBER THIS

Irving became the first American writer to achieve an international literary reputation; he was recognized in his day as the most important writer America had ever produced. His fictional creations have become American icons, as symbolic of America as Mickey Mouse, McDonald's, and machine guns. The man who missed his wake-up call, Rip Van Winkle, made success from failure to become a genuine American antihero; the Headless Horseman of Sleepy Hollow has terrified generations of trick-or-treaters (who should be home in bed anyway).

MOST FAMOUS FOR

Having as many pseudonyms as famous books. The fellow turned fifty before his real name appeared on any of his work. Here's a list of his books and pen names. See how many you can match—you will find the matchups at the end of this chapter.

Books

★ *A History of New York from the Beginning of the World to the End of the Dutch Dynasty* (1809)

★ *The Sketch Book* (1820)
★ *Bracebridge Hall* (1822)
★ *Tales of a Traveller* (1824)
★ *The Alhambra* (1832)

Pen Names

Jonathan Oldstyle, Gent.
Anthony Evergreen, Gent.
Diedrich Knickerbocker

An American Gentleman
Geoffrey Crayon

THE FATHER
OF AMERICAN LITERATURE

Washington Irving was born in New York City on April 8, 1783, the last of eleven children. (Now you know how people spent their nights before television.) Like most famous writers, he was judged a dunce as a child, but the kid understood the racket: he wrote his classmates' compositions and they did his math. When Irving was fourteen, he tried to run away to sea, having spent a year sleeping on the floor and eating slimy salt pork in preparation. His plans thwarted by alert parents, he was instead forced to attend school until he was sixteen and then sent to study law. A bout of tuberculosis resulted in a two-year tour of Europe (feel a nagging cough coming on?), but then it was back to the books. He managed to pass the bar exam in 1807 and served in a minor capacity at Aaron Burr's trial.

Around the same time, his brother William founded a satirical magazine he called *Salmagundi* (a spicy hash), enlisting Irving's help to fill its pages. Vowing to "instruct the young, reform the old, correct the town, and castigate the age," the brothers played leap-frog in the office, hoisted a few in the local bar, and even wrote a little. Having made fun of everyone they knew, the brothers suspended publication and Irving created his first great triumph, *A History of New York*, a wickedly funny spoof of various well-known figures, including President Jefferson. He launched the book with one of the cleverest hoaxes in publishing history. First, the *Evening Post* noted the disappearance of "a small elderly gentleman by the name of KNICKER-

AARON BURR (1756–1836)

Aaron Burr,
(1756–1836).
Presidential
wannabe
who made it
to Veep

Burr, the third Vice President of the United States, began his career in the Continental Army and was admitted to the New York bar in 1782. From there it was a smooth ride to attorney general and senator. In 1800 Burr served as Vice President, but four years later failed to win renomination because of Alexander Hamilton's opposition. Seriously ticked off, Burr killed Hamilton in a duel and became an instant political pariah. Washed up, he went for hung-out-to-dry by getting involved in a wild scheme to invade Spanish territory. Arrested, he was denounced for treason but was acquitted in 1807 after a six-month trial.

BOCKER." Then, a month later, another article revealed that Knickerbocker's landlord had found "a very curious kind of written book" in his lodgings, which he intended to sell to pay the back rent. At last the book appeared, credited to one "Diedrich Knickerbocker." The book made Irving a celebrity at home and abroad. A little dense, Irving did not seem to grasp that he had the right stuff, and so spent the next decade working in the family hardware business, traveling, and editing a touch. When the family business went belly-up in 1818, he turned to his pen to make a buck.

Ready for a fresh start, he went to Europe and started

creating uniquely American stories, based on old German folktales. In 1820 he published a collection of stories, *The Sketch Book*, under the pseudonym Geoffrey Crayon. Two stories in particular, "Rip Van Winkle" and "The Legend of Sleepy Hollow," catapulted him to fame, and once again Irving was head weenie at the roast.

Both his next two books, *Bracebridge Hall* (1822) and *Tales of a Traveller* (1824), were savaged by the critics, so Irving turned to biography and history, accepting an invitation to travel to Spain and work with Christopher Columbus's journals. Irving made devoted friends in Spain, as he did everywhere he went, and produced a number of books, including *History of the Life and Voyages of Columbus* (1828) and *The Alhambra* (1832), dubbed "the Spanish *Sketch Book*."

In the late 1830s, Irving bought and refurbished a charming house near Tarrytown, New York, called "Sunnyside." Lifestyle of the rich and famous can be a bore, however, and in 1842 he accepted an appointment as minister to Spain. Upon his return in 1846, the Father

Sunnyside, Washington Irving's home

of American Literature wrote a biography of the Father of His Country. He died just after finishing the last volume. More than five hundred people marched in his funeral procession; the church floor sank slightly under the unaccustomed weight of those who had crowded in for the service.

Years before his death, Irving had been recognized as a master of style as well as substance. Henry Wadsworth Longfellow and Nathaniel Hawthorne were inspired by Irving's *Sketch Book*, and their writing style owes much to his influence. Melville paid homage to Irving's genius in a late poem, ''Rip Van Winkle's Lilacs''; Charles Dickens and Sir Walter Scott acknowledged their debt to his genius. Mark Twain learned from Irving that realistic details of rural life in America could become an integral part of fiction. We owe to Irving as well the beginning of the ''local color'' school of fiction, the use of vivid details about a specific place and time. When he was not busy inspiring other writers by example, Irving was helping them in person: generous to younger writers all his life, Irving promoted Herman Melville and William Cullen Bryant, among others.

Pumpkin Head

The folks who inhabit Sleepy Hollow claim their village is bewitched. The primary ghost is the Headless Horseman, rumored to be a Hessian soldier who had lost his noggin to a stray cannonball.

Icabod Crane, a scarecrow of a man, comes to teach the village children. As was the custom, Icabod boards with each of his pupils for a week at a time. Icabod

WILLIAM CULLEN BRYANT (1794–1878)

William Cullen Bryant, 1794-1878

The backwoods bard learned Greek and Latin at his father's knee deep in the Massachusetts woods. Bryant peaked early: at nineteen he wrote the first version of his most famous poem, "Thanatopsis," a long meditation on death. Although the poem brought him immediate acclaim, only Stephen King can make a living writing, so Bryant took a law degree and became a justice of the peace. In 1825 he left the law, started a newspaper, and made a bundle. He campaigned vigorously for free speech, free trade, and abolition. He also helped organize the Republican Party, but then again, we all make mistakes.

meets Katrina Van Tassel, a looker whose substantial physical charms are augmented by her father's substantial bank account. Abraham Van Brunt, an eighteenth-century hunk, makes a formidable rival for the gaunt Icabod. Since it was tacky in the eighteenth century to assault the schoolteacher, Abraham (called Brom Bones) resorts to playing practical jokes on his rival.

The entire village is invited to a party at Mynheer Van Tassel's prosperous farm. Icabod has a wonderful time dancing with Katrina, telling ghost stories, and consuming mass quantities.

The night is dark and scary. On the way home, Icabod is shadowed by a headless horseman. Iccy races for the church bridge, where the specter is supposed to vanish in a flash of fire and brimstone. But the creature breaks with tradition and throws his head at the terrified schoolmaster.

The next morning a shattered pumpkin is found near

WHO'S WHO

"The Legend of Sleepy Hollow":
A LITERARY TOUT SHEET

Icabod Crane: The bag-of-bones schoolmaster of Sleepy Hollow, as much in love with Katrina's plump fortune as he is with her plump cheeks.

Gunpowder: Icabod's borrowed bag-of-bones horse.

Katrina Van Tassel: A rosy-cheeked rustic heiress.

Mynheer Van Tassel: Katrina's father (an early version of Daddy Warbucks).

The Headless Horseman: The legendary Hudson Valley ghost, supposedly of a Hessian cavalryman whose head had been shot off by a canonball.

Abraham Van Brunt (Brom Bones): The Alec Baldwin of the crowd, in love with lucky Katrina.

the bridge, with Icabod's horse grazing nearby. But Icabod himself is never seen again. According to tradition, Brom Bones always laughed when his wife, Katrina, told the story of the Headless Horseman who threw his head at the schoolmaster.

INQUIRING MINDS WANT TO KNOW

Today we're secure in our national identity, and our virtues—freedom, opportunity, and MTV—are trumpeted the world over. Not so in Irving's day. In the early nineteenth century, we were still a sleepy little backwater, devoid of real culture. Our tastes in books, music, and fashion were all shaped by Europe, and "Don't give up your day job" was the kind of advice you'd give an American writer. Irving put us on the literary map by showing that an American *could* write something worth reading. "The Legend of Sleepy Hollow" was among the first truly American stories, a tale set in America with American characters. Okay, so it was adapted from a German folktale and Irving wrote it while living in England; you can't have everything.

THE BIG SLEEP

Good-humored Rip Van Winkle, a kind of Norm Peterson ("Cheers") of the Kaatskill set, prefers to warm the barstool at the village inn rather than work. Although very adept at dodging his wife's messages, occa-

WHO'S HO☜

"Rip Van Winkle":
A LITERARY TOUT SHEET

Rip Van Winkle: Scion of an old Dutch family who falls asleep in the Kaatskill Mountains for twenty years.

Dame Van Winkle: Rip's wife. No wonder the man headed for the hills.

Wolf: Rip's pooch.

Judith Van Winkle: Rip's daughter.

Hendrick Hudson: Leader of the little men—munchkins on parade—who visit every twenty years to party.

sionally Rip slips up and Dame Van Winkle comes after hubby in person. When he glimpses her formidable fists, Rip heads for the hills. There, he can relax in peace.

One night on the way home from his mountain refuge, Rip is accosted by a strange little man in old-fashioned clothing who asks him to help carry a keg of liquor. At the top of the mountain, Rip finds a band of little men playing ninepins. Busy bowling for dollars, none of the little men talk with Rip. Rip takes a few snorts from the cask, and like any would-be bowling fan the world over, he falls asleep watching the game.

When Rip awakens, he looks in vain for the little

ALLEY-OOPS
. . . .
Bowling, also called "tenpins," is the second most popular game in the world, second only to soccer. A variant of the game, called "ninepins" or "skittles," is played in the Netherlands and Germany, where it seems to have originated. Dutch settlers brought the game—originally played outdoors—to America. In 1875 the National Bowling League was established in the United States, but the rules of the game were not standardized until 1895, when the American Bowling Congress was created. There are ten frames in the modern version of the game, and the highest possible score is 300.

---

men. His gun is rusty; his dog, gone. He returns to town, but no one seems to know him and his home lies in ruins. To his astonishment, Rip realizes that he has snoozed for twenty years. When he learns that his wife has died, Rip breathes a sigh of relief and lives happily ever after, regaling the locals with his strange tale. Even today, inhabitants of the village know that when they hear thunder, Hendrick Hudson and his crew are playing ninepins.

THE REAL THING

"When I first wrote 'The Legend of Rip Van Winkle,'" Irving said, "my thoughts had been for some time turned towards giving a color of romance and tradition to interesting points of our national scenery which is so generally deficient in our country." Irving succeeded so well in creating a genuine American tale that translators have always had a hard time with the story.

Henpecked husbands, overbearing wives, and mysterious apparitions remain staples of fiction. Irving's loafer-hero appeals to our taste for irresponsibility, which balances our dour puritanism. Further, the tale satirizes the notion of change. Political and social "revolutions" are superficial, Irving suggests, and real change a myth.

WHEEL OF FORTUNE

A deep well of clear water graces the front of the Alhambra. Before the days of indoor plumbing and Perrier, water carriers schlepped jars of water from the well to their customers. In Irving's story, among the best-known carriers is Pedro Gill, a hardworking and pleasant man. Although he makes a smile his umbrella, Peregil's heart is heavy: his children are ragged and hungry, and his wife is a woman who, had she lived today, would likely have been a failed disciple of diet guru Richard Simmons, and the kind of credit risk that makes second-mortgage salesmen hide in their basements.

One night Pedro encounters a dying traveler dressed like a Moor (a Muslim). Touched by the stranger's plight, Peregil brings him home. The stranger gives Peregil a small sandalwood box that he says contains a great secret. To maintain the story's suspense, he dies before he can explain the secret. Pedrillo Pedrugo, the neighbor with too much time on his hands, sees Peregil remove the body and promptly snitches to the alcalde, the law. The alcalde lets Peregil off the hook when he forks over the sandalwood box. Disappointed that it contains only a parchment scroll and candle, he takes the poor grunt's donkey instead.

A Moorish shopkeeper explains that the parchment contains an incantation for the recovery of the fabulous treasure of the Alhambra. Business has been a little slow since Peregil lost his donkey, so he goes to take a look and does indeed find a vault filled with gems and gold coins. The missus goes on a buying spree, and soon news of Peregil's windfall is hot news. The alcalde, the constable, and the prying neighbor force Peregil and the shopkeeper to go to the vault of treasure. The donkey comes along to be the ride. Peregil opens the vault and the greedy alcalde and his minions descend to fill their pockets. The Moor closes the floor over them and throws away the magic taper.

Peregil and the Moor divide the treasure between them and live happily ever after. Wouldn't you?

SPRING BREAK FROM HELL

In 1829, during his first visit to Spain, Irving lived in the Alhambra for three months. The fortress was beyond quaint: it was a ruin, stocked with assorted street people. While soaking in the sights and stench, Irving fashioned the story from scraps of legends, most notably the *Arabian Nights*. Today, in an Alhambra carefully restored for marauding bands of tourists, a marble plaque identifies the room where Irving took his ease. "The Legend of the Moor's Legacy" is also based on stock characters, including the good man, the nagging wife, the spying mischief-maker, and the corrupt ruler. So if the plot and characters are borrowed, what sets this story apart from a thousand other folktales? It's the author's skillful use of local color. (You knew that.) His details about the people and the place create a vivid, exotic realm that's romantic enough to make you reach for your AmEx card and try to book executive class to Spain. The moral of the story: It pays to do your research in person. Besides, now it's all deductible.

WHO'S H O ☞

"The Legend of the Moor's Legacy":
A LITERARY TOUT SHEET

Pedro Gill (Peregil): A poor water carrier who gets more than he expects when he helps a dying man.

His Wife: Shop-till-you-drop; she'd be a mall crawler if they'd had malls in 1832.

A Moorish Shopkeeper: Peregil's friend, skilled in languages and legends.

Pedrillo Pedrugo: The kind of neighbor who sits on a lawn chair watching your house.

The Alcalde: A Spanish mayor who values justice so highly that he sells it only for gold.

The Alhambra: The historic Spanish fortress from which the Moors had been expelled by Ferdinand and Isabella in 1492.

BEAM ME UP, SCOTTY

It's 1727. A few miles from Boston, Mr. and Mrs. Tom Walker live in wedded misery. She's a shrew who's not above aiming the plates and her right hook at hubby. But Tom's no prize either, a bum as miserly and vicious as his spouse.

One day Tom takes a shortcut through the swamp and uncovers a skull. Suddenly, a large, sooty man holding a huge ax appears and orders Tom to leave his property, but Tom refuses to be intimidated by any old armed stranger and reminds him that the land belongs to Deacon Peabody. Tom may be greedy, but he's not stupid; he quickly realizes that he's shooting the breeze with the devil himself. Having lived so long with his strong-willed wife, Tom finds the devil pleasant company and the two strike a bargain: Tom will assist the devil in exchange for the pirate Kidd's treasure. To seal the deal, the devil burns a sooty fingerprint into Tom's forehead.

DEVIL DOGS
Seems from literature that people are just lining up to sell their souls to the devil. Faust did it in Christopher Marlowe's *Dr. Faustus* (1588) and again in Goethe's *Faust* (1832). Stephen Vincent Benét picked up the theme in "The Devil and Daniel Webster" (1937); Thomas Mann contributed a remake in 1947 with *Doktor Faustus*. Even that crew-cut macho man Tab Hunter got into the act in the movie *Damn Yankees* (1958) when he tried to sell his soul to the devil (Ray Walston) in exchange for youth and a chance to play with the Yankees in the World Series. Some kids never learn.

Tom foolishly tells the missus about his strange encounter of the devilish kind, and Mrs. Walker sets out to visit the devil and cut herself in on the action. But the devil won't deal, so she returns with a bribe, the family silver. Several nights pass and Mrs. Walker does not return. Tom grows increasingly uneasy when he realizes that she has taken the silver. An eminently practical man, he says, "Let us get hold of the property, and we will endeavor to do without the woman." He finds nothing but her heart and liver tied up in her apron. Tom consoles himself for the loss of his silver with the cheering news that he has lost his unbeloved wife as well. Tom and the devil subsequently meet to work out the fine points of their deal. Tom becomes a moneylender, gleefully foreclosing and dispossessing.

Seeing the end approaching, Tom embraces religion as a shield against damnation. He's fine until he shouts out, "The devil take me if I have made a farthing!" The devil, an obliging chap, calls in his chit.

GOING TO THE DEVIL

"The Devil and Tom Walker," from *Tales of a Traveller*, is based on a German folktale about a man who sells his soul to the devil. Irving makes the tale distinctly American by switching the setting to New England in 1727, just as the Puritan belief that the life that should be devoted to God was being replaced by commercialism and materialism. The story satirizes hypocritical Puritans who used their prominence to amass wealth; images of darkness and rot contrast with the seeming solidity of pious professions like the clergy. As with all of Irving's best works, "The Devil and Tom Walker" starts with the ludicrous and builds to the fearful. The Gothic props— the devil, the dank forest, the grisly killing—help make a legend out of something ordinary in the American experience.

WHO'S WHO 👉

"The Devil and Tom Walker":
A LITERARY TOUT SHEET

Tom Walker: Makes Scrooge look like a Mr. Generosity.

Mrs. Walker: A little more than kin but less than kind; Leona Helmsley—with the attitude.

Old Scratch: A devil of a fellow.

SUMMARY

⏱ Wrote celebrated short stories, satires, travel books.

⏱ Sparked local-color writing, vivid details about a specific place and time.

⏱ Paved the way for the development of the historical novel (which has devolved in our time into a justifiably underrated genre, airport fiction).

⏱ Possessed considerable personal charm and generosity, astonishing traits in a writer.

James Fenimore Cooper, 1789-1851

CHAPTER 2

JAMES FENIMORE COOPER

(1789–1851)

YOU MUST REMEMBER THIS

Cooper copped a lot of firsts, creating the first American adventure story, the first American novel of manners, and the first American novel of the sea. With all this, Cooper became the first successful American novelist.

MOST FAMOUS FOR

Action-packed plots and his macho frontiersman, Natty Bumppo, one of the best-known characters in world literature. Cooper's fame rests largely on *The Leatherstocking Tales,* a series of five novels about Natty Bumppo: *The Pioneers* (1823), *The Last of the Mohicans* (1826), *The Prairie* (1827), *The Pathfinder* (1840), and *The Deerslayer* (1841). But when he wasn't suing some neighbor or another, he also wrote a lot of other good stuff, including:

★ *The Spy* (1821)
★ *The Pilot* (1823)
★ *The Red Rover* (1827)
★ *A Letter to His Countrymen* (1834)

★ *Satanstoe* (1845)
★ *The Chainbearer* (1845)
★ *The Redskins* (1846)

THE AMERICAN SCOTT

On his deathbed, Cooper begged his family not to allow any account of his life to be published. Likely this was because Cooper realized that he had raised tactlessness to an art form, and feared that posterity might not overlook his insufferable snobbery, litigious nature, and general crankiness while praising his genius. During his long life, Cooper managed to insult an astonishingly wide range of people on both sides of the Atlantic. Arriving in London, for example, he announced that the majestic Thames River was "a stream of trivial expanse." At home he spent his nonwriting time slandering and suing his neighbors. He was, as the twentieth-century writer D. H. Lawrence put it, "a gentleman in the worst sense."

Nothing in Cooper's early life prepared him to be such a grouch. When Cooper was thirteen months old, his affable and astute father moved his considerable clan from Burlington, New Jersey, to the shores of Otsego Lake in central New York. Flatly refusing to leave civilization for the wilderness, Mrs. Cooper plopped herself firmly in her armchair. Mr. Cooper hoisted her, armchair and all, into the wagon and headed north. William Cooper settled his wife, her armchair, and his seven children on more than half a million acres. With characteristic family modesty, he named his spread "Cooperstown."

Although a wealthy country squire of the first order, Cooper *père* had the common touch, settling arguments with a friendly wrestling match and spreading around the brewski in lieu of cash. Under his father's good-natured guidance, young Cooper flour-

COOPERSTOWN

Although we folks in the book biz like to think that Cooperstown is famous as the home of James Fenimore Cooper, the grim reality is that our man in the forest has been overshadowed by the overhyped national pastime. While intrepid literature majors still trek to Cooperstown to soak in the leftover ink, most traffic in that quaint tourist trap can be attributed to a nonliterary landmark, the National Baseball Hall of Fame and Museum. In 1839, while Cooper was inventing the American novel, Abner Doubleday was supposedly inventing a minor sport called baseball. If you're in the neighborhood and want to stop by the Baseball Hall of Fame after prostrating yourself at the foot of the Cooper monument, you will find that the museum houses a ton of baseball memorabilia and a gallery of bronze plaques honoring the nation's outstanding players.

Baseball Hall of Fame in Cooperstown, New York

ished. The child was such an outstanding student, in fact, that he entered Yale in 1803, when he was only thirteen years old. Although he was a "fine, sparkling" lad, as one of his professors later noted, young Cooper was not above a prank or two. School officials overlooked it when he ran up huge debts in fashionable shops and blew off a classmate's door with gunpowder, but they had trouble ignoring the donkey Cooper taught to sit in a professor's chair. Out on his ear, the lad returned to the family mansion.

Correctly surmising that he was a little lax in the discipline department, Cooper senior decided that his youngest son needed a firm hand and promptly sent him to sea. In October of 1806, Cooper set sail aboard the *Stirling*, a small merchant ship bound out of New York for England with a load of flour.

Barely seventeen years old, Cooper took his place on deck next to kindly old salts screaming with delirium tremens. The voyage was uneventful—the usual pursuit by a heavily armed pirate ship, attempted impressment by the British Navy, and various men overboard. Two years later Cooper had learned the ropes well enough to get his midshipman's certificate, signed by Thomas Jefferson. The lad was hot to check out the beaches and nightlife in warmer climates, and so was bitterly disappointed when he was assigned to an inactive bomb ketch laid up for repairs in New York Harbor. Things got even worse with his next assignment: Oswego, a frontier village on Lake Ontario, two hundred miles from the sea. Fate intervened, and Cooper abandoned his first love, the sea, for his second, Susan DeLancey, an heiress who was winsome as well as loaded. During their courtship Cooper's father died, leaving his son $50,000 and a share in the $750,000 estate. Susan and James married in 1811, only after he promised to give up his naval career. At first the marriage was happy as well as prosperous, producing four daughters along with frequent interest checks. But in the depression following the War of 1812, the Cooper family fortune collapsed. To make matters worse, Cooper's five profligate brothers died between 1813 and 1819, leaving Cooper to support their large families. As the new paterfamilias, he begged and borrowed in a vain attempt to keep the clan afloat.

According to family legend, Cooper was reading a new novel from England when he threw it aside and exclaimed, "I could write a better book than that myself!" Susan challenged him to make good his boast; the following year he completed *Precaution* (1820). The critics objected that it was little more than another echo of English fiction, so Cooper once again rose to the taunt, this time producing two undeniably American books: *The Spy*, a tale of the American Revolution, and *The Pioneers*, a runaway bestseller about the frontier. The later sold 3,500 copies on the morning of its first day in print. When

Sir Walter Scott,
1771-1832

people at a dinner party praised Sir Walter Scott's latest sea story, Cooper churned out *The Pilot*, the first of his eleven influential sea stories. Critics accorded him the highest praise they could, dubbing him "the American Scott" and likening his thrilling yarns to the spellbinding stories of Britain's Sir Walter. While neither man liked the comparison, it sold books. Cooper's money problems were over.

In 1826 Cooper added the "Fenimore" to his name

WANTED: A REAL *AMERICAN* NOVEL

Although today America is a happening kind of place thanks to Cameros, MTV, and McDonald's, our forbears were considered little more than unlettered barbarians. "Who reads an American book?" critics sneered. Master of gothic horror Charles Brockden Brown and political satirist Hugh Henry Brackenridge had given it their best shot, but their ambitions exceeded their talents. Washington Irving had disappointed many by limiting himself to the short story. Cooper sailed to the rescue, salvaging American honor by creating the first full-length epic from American settings and characters. "Cooper," said one reviewer, "laid the foundations for American literature."

to honor his mother's family, set off for Europe with his own family, and during the seven years he was there managed to alienate most of the civilized world. His spoken and written criticism was distributed with admirable impartiality; few persons or places could complain they had been overlooked. In an attempt to defend himself against attacks by the press and public, Cooper published *A Letter to His Countrymen*, which served only to arouse more bad feelings. Back home, he continued to write, and began a series of lawsuits against his neighbors for picnicking on his land. His awesome productivity and litigation continued unabated through the years, and he wrote and sued until he could no longer hold a pen. In 1851 he died. His reputation declined in the late 1800s, was revived in the 1920s, and continues unabated today.

WHAT'S
H
A
T
☛

The Leatherstocking Tales:
A LITERARY TOUT SHEET

Each of the five books of *The Leatherstocking Tales* traces one phase in the life and times of frontiersman Natty Bumppo, the last action hero of the New World. Raised by Indians, Bumppo is a deer-clad Superman, faster than a speeding bullet, more powerful than a locomotive, and able to race-walk fifty miles without stopping to take a breath. Natty's nickname changes with his age and locale. Since the books were written out of chronological order, here's a handy-dandy crib sheet to help you keep them straight:

Title	Date of Publication	Date of Action	Natty Bumppo's Name	Natty Bumppo's Age
The Deerslayer	1841	1740s	Deerslayer	early 20s
The Last of the Mohicans	1826	1757	Hawkeye	mid-30s
The Pathfinder	1840	1759	Pathfinder	late 30s
The Pioneers	1823	1793	Leatherstocking	early 70s
The Prairie	1827	1804	"the trapper" or "the old man"	80s

BUMPP AND GRIND

Cora and Alice Munro, Colonel Munro's comely daughters, are trekking through the wilderness to their father's headquarters at Fort William Henry. Major Duncan Heyward, a young British officer, and David Gamut, a singing teacher, have come along for the ride. They are guided by Magua, a treacherous Huron who claims he knows the shortcut. Hawkeye and his two Delaware friends, Chingachgook and his son, Uncas, happen by and mention casually that Magua has been leading the group in a circle. Realizing that the jig is up, Magua heads for

WHO'S
H
O ☞

The Last of the Mohicans:
A LITERARY TOUT SHEET

Natty Bumppo, called "Hawkeye": The long, lean hunk straight from central casting; no Wuss of the West here, folks.

Chingachgook: The courageous and loyal Mohican chief; Hawkeye's main man.

Uncas: The last of the Mohicans; Chingachgook's stalwart son. Looking for love in all the wrong places, he falls for Cora, and she for him.

Major Duncan Heyward: Like many other men in this book, handsome, clever, brave, loyal, etc.

WHO'S
H
O
☛

(Continued)

Magua: The macho, clever, brave . . . renegade Huron chief who seeks to avenge himself on Colonel Munro by turning his feisty daughter, Cora, into a servile squaw.

Cora Munro: The dishy dark-haired daughter, equally handy with a flintlock and a frying pan.

Alice Munro: Cora's half sister, the pale flower of womanhood who clings like the high-priced plastic wrap.

Colonel Munro: Ultimately unsuccessful in defending Fort William Henry, but gives it the ol' Revolutionary try.

David Gamut: The sole milquetoast of the group, a singing teacher steeped in schoolbook piety.

The Marquis de Montcalm: The enterprising French general who captures Fort William Henry and allows the Hurons to massacre the defeated English; definitely off the Christmas card list.

General Webb: Fort Edward's incompetent commander; straight out of "F Troop."

the hills. Hostile Huron warriors attack. Wild pursuit! A hairbreath 'scape! The good guys abandon their horses and hide in a cave. Their ammunition gone, Cora, in a voice with more timbre than Yellowstone National Park, takes over and insists that Hawkeye and his buddies seek help. With Our Hero gone, Magua and his men capture Cora, Alice, Heyward, and Gamut. Cora sneers, tossing her silky raven tresses and is promptly tied to a stake in preparation for torture. Pan to lush scenery as the music rises to a crescendo.

Mr. Large and Reliable to the rescue! He blasts the Indians with his trusted rifle, called "Killdeer," and saves the day. In the melee, Magua slips away. Our Hero takes the gang to Fort William Henry, fools the guard by speaking flawless French, and enters the fort. The English surrender the fort and the Iroquois attack. Magua

COOPER MAKES THE BIG SCREEN

The Last of the Mohicans has spawned a number of film versions. Its most recent incarnation (1992, 20th Century Fox) transforms the jolly good adventure tale into a jolly good romance. Daniel Day-Lewis plays Hawkeye and romances his Cora, Madeleine Stowe, amid lots of brutal conflict and majestic mountains. In 1977 director James L. Conway cast Steve Forrest and Ned Romero in a lukewarm version. The most satisfying flick remains George B. Seitz's 1936 foray, starring Randolph Scott as the intrepid Hawkeye, Robert Barrat as the noble Chingachgook, and Binnie Barnes as virginal Alice Munro. Lots and lots of blood and thunder.

grabs Alice and Cora and flees. Hawkeye and his buddies set off to find them.

At the Huron camp, they learn the women are nearby. Aided by Hawkeye, Duncan rescues his beloved Alice. The Delawares, led by Uncas, Hawkeye, and Chingachgook, defeat the Iroquois, but Cora is stabbed by a Huron and Magua kills Uncas. Hawkeye and his noble sidekick Chingachgook survive for the sequel.

SO WHY NOT JUST WATCH THE MOVIE?

The novel, unlike the movie, shows how Cooper interprets the American experience and elevates it to epic level. Cooper makes Uncas's death typify the tragedy of the Native American encounter with the white man, giving the work a heroic significance. His characters show the origin of the qualities that define America: bravery, self-reliance, and democracy. By creating a fable that combines the universal Western myth of the Noble Savage with a direct knowledge of the American frontier, Cooper expresses the grandeur of that frontier. That's why you should read the book. Besides, it's cheaper and less fattening than all that buttered popcorn.

SON OF BESTSELLER STALKS THE FOREST

The novel opens with Natty traveling with Hurry Harry to meet Chingachgook at Lake Glimmerglass. At Muskrat

WHO'S WHO ☞

The Deerslayer:
A LITERARY TOUT SHEET

Hurry Harry March: A ferocious, greedy frontiersman, an in-your-face kind of guy.

Tom Hutter: Yo-ho-ho! Former pirate turns trapper to evade the law. Left no forwarding address.

Judith Hutter: Tom's daughter. Looking for love in all the wrong places, this chick's too hot for the frontier.

Hetty Hutter: Judith's sister. Her Christian simplicity awes even the Indians and they grant her safe passage.

Hist-ho!-Hist or **Wah-ta!-Wah:** Chingachgook's main squeeze, called by either name.

Captain Warley: The cavalry to the rescue; the savvy commander of the troops that save Our Hero.

Rivenoak: The enemy Iroquois chief, fierce but honorable.

Natty Bumppo (called "Deerslayer"): Our man in the forest.

Chingachgook: His noble main man.

Castle, Harry makes a play for the owner's saucy daughter, Judith. But she falls for a British officer and thus breaks the moral code of her day. In the meantime, Hurry Harry and Hutter harvest some Indian scalps and are captured by their intended victims, the Mingos. Deerslayer waits for Chingachgook, who is on a mission to rescue Hist from the enemy Iroquois. Deerslayer meets with the Iroquois chief Rivenoak to ransom Hurry Harry and Hutter.

When Deerslayer and HH reach Glimmerglass, they find that the Mingos have already arrived on the scene. Unfortunately for Our Hero and his sidekick, the Native Americans are not happy about this intrusion into their territory. Natty, HH, and Chingachgook join forces with the Hutters to rescue the lovely Hist. Their quest is successful, which naturally makes the Mingos more annoyed. To make their anger quite clear, the Mingos take Natty prisoner. Hutter and HH are recaptured while seeking scalps; in a delicious bit of irony, Hutter himself is scalped. After confessing that he is not the girls' father, Hutter dies. Deerslayer joins the Iroquois and is promptly tortured. Chingachgook to the rescue! The cavalry thunders down the hill, stirs up a lot of dust, and slaughters all the Indians. Along the way, Hetty is killed. Judith goes off to wicked Europe (where everyone does the two-step with everyone else) as the mistress of the British officer who first seduced her. Fifteen years later Deerslayer and Chingachgook return to find the castle in ruins.

THE IROQUOIS
. . . .

*Hendrick, Chief
of the Mohawks*

The Iroquois Confederacy included five tribes—Mohawk, Onondaga, Cayuga, Oneida, and Seneca—known as the Five Nations. A complex and stable political organization, combined with skill in warfare, enabled the Iroquois to become very powerful during the seventeenth century. By 1720 they had conquered almost all the tribes from the Atlantic to the Mississippi, from the St. Lawrence to the Tennessee River. Cooper lived too late to know many Indians personally; although he romanticized them, he did not falsify. What Cooper noted in the Native Americans were their acute senses, developed through woodcraft and warfare, their belief in omens, their stoicism when undergoing torture, their respect for the feeble and aged, their eloquence in oratory, and their fierce tribal pride.

INQUIRING MINDS WANT TO KNOW

The Deerslayer is much more than an edge-of-the-seat adventure tale. Cooper makes every incident dramatize his characters' moral attitudes. Although these passages can be a real snooze, the moral stance of his novels is what gives them power. Natty Bumppo becomes the representative hero of a culture that blends qualities the Europeans brought to the New World with the qualities of the frontier.

Judith is the prototype of the Fallen Woman. Her type

*"The Bambi Brigade, an animal rights group
is here to see you about the Deerslayer, Mr. Cooper."*

reappears as head-of-the-class Hester Prynne in Nathaniel Hawthorne's *Scarlet Letter* and later as Charlotte Stant, the brilliant adventuress in Henry James's *Golden Bowl.*

THE SPY WHO LOVED ME
GOES TO SEA

You've read it before, folks: Cooper converted land skirmishes into chases between frigates and men-of-war. Drawn-out love scenes alternate with brief escapades, as

the Tory captain and the larger-than-life Jones are captured, released, and recaptured; finally, the elder Howard
is wounded and consents to the marriage of his attractive

WHO'S WHO

The Pilot:

A LITERARY TOUT SHEET

Mr. Gray (John Paul Jones): Betrayed by the
Brits, the pilot of the title switches to the American team.

Lt. Richard Barnstable: The reckless officer of
the schooner *Ariel* who carries a torch for
Katherine.

Edward Griffith: The bold yet sensible
lieutenant.

Colonel Howard: Exiled American Tory living
in England.

Christopher (Kit) Dillon: Part of the heavy-
cufflink crowd, out for himself.

Long Tom Coffin: Stouthearted sailor who
thwarts Dillon's dastardly schemes.

Katherine Plowden: Colonel Howard's ward
and niece.

Cecilia Howard: Colonel Howard's niece and
Griffith's love.

ward to a Yankee. Throughout the story, Jones's personality is shrouded in mystery. He is a moody Scotsman, but always ready to spring into action. Reader affection goes to resourceful old salt from Nantucket, Long Tom Coffin.

The Pilot was to have many imitators, but none surpassed its thrilling action on the sea. But Cooper did more than create a thumping good tale. For the first time in prose, an author expressed the mystery, challenge, and downright sexiness of the briny deep. In the sea's dark face we feel the press of eternity and faith. Cooper evoked in his readers an emotional response to the ocean, the same feeling Herman Melville and Joseph Conrad would create years later.

The Prairie

Natty Bumppo, now an aged trapper and frontiersman, saves an immigrant train from an Indian raid, and after several escapades with the Sioux, a prairie fire, and a buffalo stampede, he finds refuge for his last days with the troops of Captain Middleton, the grandson of his old friend Duncan Heyward, and with the friendly Pawnees. Cooper had never been to the West and, as a matter of fact, wrote the book in a Paris boardinghouse. As a result, the text does not exactly emit the heady aroma of saddle sweat. Nonetheless, the novel concludes the Leatherstocking series on a note of spiritual elevation.

A DO-IT-YOURSELF COOPER NOVEL:
CREATE YOUR OWN PLOT
IN ONE SENTENCE

Take one or more from each column to create your own Cooper novel. Some of the combinations may seem odd, but take heart: Cooper would have written *your* plot eventually.

SETTINGS
amidst virgin forests
amidst heaving ocean
amidst besieged forts
amidst Lake Glimmerglass

HEROES
manly pioneers
manly Indians
demure blond debs
brunette spitfires

VILLAINS
confront dastardly sailors
confront dastardly Indians
confront dastardly soldiers

WEAPONS
armed with swords
armed with muskets
armed with bows and arrows

SUMMARY

🕰 Created the first American adventure novel, the first American novel of manners, and the first novel of the sea.

🕰 Raised the American frontier experience to epic proportions and helped define the American character.

🕰 Produced some of literature's most famous characters, including Natty Bumppo, Chingachgook, and Uncas.

🕰 Crafted hold-on-to-your-seats adventure tales.

*Henry David Thoreau, 1817-1862,
Naturalist and writer*

CHAPTER 3

THE
TRANSCENDENTALISTS

YOU MUST REMEMBER THIS

The Transcendentalists, led by Ralph Waldo Emerson and Henry David Thoreau, celebrated individualism, worshipped nature, and embraced intuition. They gave the hippies of the 1970s a raison d'être and set the stage for the New Age crystal queens.

MOST FAMOUS FOR

Emerson batted it out of the park with his essays and made it to second base with his poems; Thoreau hit a home run with *Walden*. Here's a list of their best work:

Ralph Waldo Emerson (1803–1882)
★ *Nature* (1836)
★ *Essays, First Series* (1841)
★ *Essays, Second Series* (1844)
★ *Poems* (1847)
★ *Representative Men* (1850)
★ *Conduct of Life* (1860)
★ *Journals* (10 volumes)

Henry David Thoreau (1817–1862)
★ *Walden, or, Life in the Woods* (1854)
★ "Civil Disobedience" (1849)
★ *A Week on the Concord and Merrimack Rivers* (1849)
★ *Journals* (16 volumes)

THE TRANSCENDENTALISTS

Like the 1969 musical love-in at Woodstock, the nineteenth-century Transcendental movement was brief, messy, and influential out of all proportion to its size. The Transcendental party kicked off in 1836 with the formation of the Transcendental Club in Boston. Key players included Emerson, Thoreau, feminist Margaret Fuller, preacher Theodore Parker, educator Bronson Alcott, and philosopher William Ellery Channing. The group published a little magazine, *The Dial*, and some of the members got a little closer together at Brook Farm, a commune that set the pace for all coed dorms to follow.

The Transcendentalists saw a direct connection, or "correspondence," between the universe and the individual soul. By contemplating objects in nature, they believed, individuals can transcend the world and discover

Roughin' it with the Transcendentalists

MARGARET FULLER (1810–1850)

Margaret Fuller, 1810-1850, Brenda Starr of the Transcendental set

As the Brenda Starr of the Transcendental set, Fuller had the distinction of being our first self-supporting female journalist. A groundbreaking advocate for social reform, Fuller had a tempestuous love affair with a young Italian nobleman and gave birth to their son in secret, without a pause in her news dispatches. She, her lover, and their infant son died in a shipwreck off Fire Island, New York. The baby's body washed ashore, but Thoreau searched in vain for Fuller's remains. Though she was depicted during her life as alternately sex-starved and sex-crazed, her writings reveal a brilliant mind and brave social reformer.

union with the Over-Soul, also known as the Ideal or Supreme Mind. The trick, these people believed, is to follow the sway of your own beliefs, however divergent from the social norm they may be. Since all people are inherently good, the mantra ran, the individual's intuitive response to any given situation will be the right thing to do.

THE SAGE OF CONCORD: RALPH WALDO EMERSON

Ralph Waldo Emerson, 1803-1882, Dean of American Transcendentalists

Happily married, good to dogs and kids, the kind of guy you'd call for a lift to the train station, Emerson led a totally upright and conventional life. Nonetheless, every American writer of his era—and every American writer to follow—has had to come to terms with his legacy, and the reactions have varied wildly. On one end of the scale, Herman Melville in *The Confidence Man* brutally mocked him as a philosophical fraud; on the other, Thoreau, Walt Whitman, and Emily Dickinson worshiped him as the fount of inspiration. His influence is evident in the novels of Theodore Dreiser and the poems of Robert Frost and Wallace Stevens, to name just a few.

Emerson was eight years old when his father, a Unitarian minister, died. Determined that her four sons would attend Harvard, Mrs. Emerson converted her home to a boardinghouse in order to afford the tuition. Although a mensch early on, Emerson was nonetheless an average scholar. After graduation he tried his hand at teaching, escaping four years later into divinity school. He celebrated his ordainment at twenty-six by marrying Ellen Tucker, who died less than two years later from tuberculosis. Grief-stricken, he turned in his cassock and set off for Europe to Find Himself.

UNITARIANISM

Unitarianism is the form of Christianity that denies the doctrines of the Trinity, original sin, vicarious atonement, the deity of Jesus Christ, and everlasting punishment. So what's left? you may ask. Well, you have the Eucharist and infant baptism, but the Transcendentalists felt that that just wasn't enough religion. The whole brouhaha over Transcendentalism started around 1820, when a group of young Unitarian ministers agitated that the party line had become too rational and lacked the essentials of a religious experience: intuition, emotion, and mystery. "It's a jumping-off place from the church to absolute infidelity," one minister complained. And Transcendentalism, a new -ism, was born.

When a legacy from his wife's estate granted him financial freedom, Emerson returned home, remarried, and began writing. His first pamphlet, *Nature*, did little to establish his literary reputation, at least in part because it was anonymous. Nonetheless, this publication did become the unofficial manifesto of the Transcendental Club and made his friends happy. His speech to Harvard's Divinity School graduates in 1838 was a different matter. In his oration Emerson declared that true religion resides within the individual, not in Christianity or in the church. Since everyone has equal access to the Divine Spirit, all that people need in order to validate religious truth is their inner experience. This did not sit well with a flock of freshly minted ministers who had just spent the best years of their lives locked in a stuffy classroom learning theology. Emerson the infidel was barred from speaking at his alma mater for thirty years.

Emerson's fame grew when *Essays* shot to the top of the charts in 1841 and made him the unofficial prophet from Massachusetts. Unlike Henry David Thoreau, his cantankerous homeboy and sometime handyman, Emerson was a convivial and generous fellow who enjoyed a wide circle of friends. When his house burned to the ground in 1877, his friends and admirers sent him on an all-expenses-paid visit to Europe and Egypt. The house was rebuilt in his absence—at their expense. His mind collapsed before his body, and he spent the last decade of his life in benign senility, beloved as a prophet of individualism, idealism, optimism, and self-confidence.

NATURE

This long essay is Emerson's I'm-okay-you're-okay hymn to individualism, in which he explains how nature's leafy bosom can restore our confidence and release our powers, as religion once did. The basic concept: Nature is God's working made visible to humanity. "The whole of nature is a metaphor of the human mind. . . . This relation between the mind and matter is not fancied by some poets, but stands in the will of God, and so is free to be known by all men." Got that? It follows, then, that the way to God's truth is by communing with nature, not through reason. This works especially well if you failed math but did okay in earth science.

EPIGRAM HELL
. . . .
Since Emerson and Thoreau knew how to turn a phrase, their philosophy has become reduced to aphorisms that fit neatly on birthday cards. Here are their top ten quotes, which you've likely encountered shopping for a card for that special someone, like Ralph Waldo Emerson.

Emerson:
1. "Speak your latent conviction, and it shall be the universal sense."
2. "Society everywhere is in conspiracy against the manhood of every one of its members."
3. "Nothing is at last sacred but the integrity of your own mind."
4. "My life is for itself and not a spectacle."
5. "A foolish consistency is the hobgoblin of little minds,/Adored by little statesmen and philosophers and divines."
6. "An institution is the lengthened shadow of one man."
7. "Life only avails, not the having lived."

Thoreau:
8. "That government is best which governs not at all."
9. "If a man does not keep pace with his companions, perhaps it is because he hears a different drummer. Let him step to the music which he hears, however measured or far away."
10. "The mass of men lead lives of quiet desperation."

Nature not only reveals truths; it also disciplines people by rewarding them when it is used properly and punishing them when it is abused. You know what this means: we're in big trouble today.

"You have a blessed Henry David Thoreau quote for everything!"

"THE AMERICAN SCHOLAR"

Emerson delivered "The American Scholar" before the Phi Beta Kappa Society in 1837. "Our intellectual Declaration of Independence," Oliver Wendell Holmes, Sr., deemed Emerson's thunderous address. In his speech Emerson called for distinctively American writing, free from European influence. It was a call for Americans to trust their individuality and act as noble representatives to the world. Its effect was not unlike that of God delivering the tablets to Moses.

The main influences on the scholar's education are nature, books, and action, Emerson declared. Scholars

OLIVER WENDELL HOLMES, SR. (1809–1894)

Oliver Wendell Holmes, 1809-1894, physician, writer, and autocrat

Writer and physician Holmes was a quintessential Boston Brahmin, a member of that insular town's high (WASP) society. In his spare time (when not publishing landmark medical studies and lecturing at Harvard Medical School), he turned out entertaining essays and insightful poems. He hit it big as a writer in 1857 with *The Autocrat of the Breakfast Table*, a series of witty essays published first in the influential *Atlantic Monthly*. His poems are standardtextbook fare: you might have encountered "Old Ironsides" (1830) or "The Chambered Nautilus" (1858) in English 101. His son, Oliver Wendell Holmes, Jr. (the family's imagination did not run to names), was a distinguished Supreme Court justice.

who are free and brave will be rewarded amply: their mind will be altered by the truths they discover. And you thought better living came through chemistry. "The ancient precept, 'Know thyself,' and the modern precept, 'Study nature,' become at last one maxim," he reasoned.

"SELF-RELIANCE"

Picking up where the Phi Beta Kappa speech left off, Emerson declared, "Whoso would be a man, must be a nonconformist.'' Holds for women, too. If nature reveals the moral truths of life, then people must focus on nature, humanity, and humanity's attitude toward nature. Only the person brave enough to go it alone will discover the truth, although the truth is apparent to anyone who looks. When you find truth, you will see what binds all people. "To believe your own thought, to believe that what is true for you in your private heart is true for all men—that is genius.''

So he sounds like a hopeless dreamer. The problem is that Emerson really did try to live the life he extolled, but it took Thoreau to make it work. What did Emerson accomplish? He gave stirring expression to the American faith in the creative capacity of the individual soul.

"HYMN SUNG AT THE COMPLETION OF THE CONCORD MONUMENT, APRIL 19, 1836''

This is one of Emerson's most popular poems, probably because it's a real toe-tapper. It was composed for the dedication of a monument to those who fought at the Battle of Concord, and so follows a predictable pattern. After summarizing the past occasion, the poem comments on the passage of time between the past and present and then concludes on a suitably inspiring note.

Although Emerson wrote relatively little poetry, he made up in impact what he lacked in bulk. He was the first to define what made American poetry American— verse that celebrated ordinary experience rather than epic themes and focused on facts rather than on eloquence. The maker of this democratic verse would be equal parts prophet, oracle, visionary, and seer. Scorning imitators, he would demand freshness and originality, even though he could rarely deliver in his own verse what he demanded from others. But when Emerson rang the bell, as with this poem, it rang clear and true. His poems try to accomplish what his essays declare: the joining of people and nature.

Like a good hunting dog, Emerson pointed the way, but it remained for Whitman to bag the prey. To his credit, Emerson was among the first (and only) to jump on Whitman's bandwagon.

HENRY DAVID THOREAU

To his neighbors, Henry was a washout: a Harvard graduate who seemed to spend his days loafing. When he wasn't wandering aimlessly through the woods, he was home writing; every now and again he'd help out at his father's pencil factory. After a brief stint teaching, he worked off and on as Emerson's handyman; he did a little surveying when he ran short of cash. Occasionally he earned twenty-five dollars or so for lecturing in small towns—charming audiences with his Yankee wit, instructing them on ecology—or lecturing on the evils of slavery. He never married, and had no lover of either sex. From 1845 to 1847, he lived near Walden Pond in a small cabin that he built himself. At his own expense, Thoreau printed 1,000 copies of his first book, *A Week on the Concord and Merrimack Rivers*; 275 books sold, the rest served as attic insulation. His second book, *Walden*, wasn't a boffo bestseller, either: a total of 7 copies sold, most of them to his mother. Even Emerson, his closest

ROMANTICISM

Transcendentalism was an offshoot of the Romantic movement then sweeping across Europe. Shaped by the French Revolution and the effects of the Industrial Revolution, the Romantics desired radical change, idolized the individual and the common people, and obsessed over nature. Such Romantics as Wordsworth, Coleridge, Keats, and Shelley focused on emotion and imagination and sought to develop new forms of expression. Also interested in the supernatural and the mysterious, they tended toward excess and spontaneity.

friend, thought that Thoreau was drifting through life, but he did buy a copy of both his books.

But Thoreau was not drifting. Rather, his entire life was a deliberate attempt to live precisely the way he wanted. While the world expected one definition of success, Thoreau lived another, and his writing won for itself a permanence that belied the opinion of his contemporaries. Thoreau acted out the dictates of his conscience with a determination unsettling to those living more cautious lives. For example, while Emerson and most others were holding themselves aloof from the slavery problem, Thoreau was helping runaway slaves escape to Canada. Thoreau became the first American to speak in defense of John Brown, delivering his fiery "Plea for Captain John Brown" in 1859.

Thoreau died from tuberculosis at the age of forty-four. According to one story, a few hours before his death an aunt asked, "Henry, have you made your peace with God?" Thoreau replied, "I did not know that we had quarreled." Another witness claims he said, "Moose." Take your pick.

JOHN BROWN (1800–1859)

John Brown, 1800-1859, fiery abolitionist

Actively hostile to slavery all his life, in 1855 Brown followed his five sons to Kansas Territory, the epicenter of the pro- and antislavery struggle. Under his leadership, the family took arms against marauding proslavery terrorists from Missouri who had murdered a group of abolitionists. On May 14, 1856, Brown and his sons avenged the murders by killing five proslavery agitators. Emboldened by his success, Brown framed a plan to free the slaves by armed force. He launched his attack on October 16, 1859, by seizing the U.S. Arsenal at Harpers Ferry, Virginia. The militia, led by Robert E. Lee, marched in and killed ten of Brown's twenty-one men. Charged and convicted of treason and murder, Brown was hanged on December 2. Catapulted to martyrdom, he became the subject of the federal soldiers' marching son, "John Brown," whose "body lies a-mouldering in the grave" and "soul goes marching on."

By the 1930s Thoreau had gained the status of a major American writer; in the next decades he attained a higher rank than Emerson. In his writing, nature and narrator become one, and the ecological and the spiritual unite.

Walden

"Simplicity, simplicity, simplicity! I say, let your affairs be as two or three, and not a hundred or a thousand; instead of a million count half a dozen, and keep your accounts on your thumbnail." It's a passage to make a capitalist shudder. Worst of all, Thoreau meant every word of it.

Walden is a Fodor's for the mind, a book that shows you how to live wisely in a world designed to make wise living impossible. Chock-a-block with brief fables, allegories, aphorisms, and puns, *Walden* shows you that happiness can be yours if you're willing to throw away the Rolex, the Armani wardrobe, and the Lexus and grow your own beans.

Never one to overlook an omen, Thoreau moved into the tiny cabin at Walden Pond on July 4, 1845, making his own personal declaration of independence

Walden Pond

E. B. WHITE ON *WALDEN*

In 1954 E. B. White (essayist and author of the children's arachno-classic *Charlotte's Web*) wrote an article in honor of the hundredth anniversary of the publication of *Walden*. "*Walden* is an oddity in American letters," he wrote. "It may very well be the oddest of our distinguished oddities. . . . Many think it a sermon; many set it down as an attempt to rearrange society; some think it an exercise in nature-loving; some find it a rather irritating collection of inspirational puffballs by an eccentric showoff. I think it none of these. It still seems to me the best youth's companion yet written by an American, for it carries a solemn warning against the loss of one's valuables, it advances a good argument for traveling light and trying new adventures, it rings with the power of positive adoration, it contains religious feelings without religious images, and it steadfastly refuses to record bad news."

from materialism. The move enabled him to commune with nature and devote more time to his writing. But he realized life in the woods might not be everyone's cup of joe: "If a man does not keep pace with his companions, perhaps it is because he hears a different drummer. Let him step to the music which he hears, however measured or far away." With the iron ax comes an iron will.

"CIVIL DISOBEDIENCE"

From 1846 to 1848, the United States had a nasty little spat with Mexico over the boundary between Mexico and

Texas and over Mexico's stubborn refusal to sell us those tasty morsels California and New Mexico. Thoreau strongly objected to the war on several fronts, not the least being his belief that President Polk had lit the powder keg before getting Congress's approval. Thoreau knew that the way to a government's heart is through its wallet, so he withheld his taxes to show *his* disapproval. To show *its* disapproval, the government slapped Henry in jail. He was a minor annoyance, however, so he spent only one night in the lockup. Emerson visited Thoreau on his day in jail and asked, "Henry, why are you here?" Thoreau answered, "Waldo, why are you *not* here?" No one ever said that Henry was an easy friend.

From this experience came the essay "Civil Disobedience," in which Thoreau makes the case that there will never be a true government until the individual is recognized as a higher and independent power from which all authority is derived. "Government is at best but an expedient," he believed. And: "That government is best which governs not at all."

The essay had a tremendous effect on the oppressed the world over. In 1906 Mahatma Gandhi made "Civil Disobedience" the major document in the struggle for Indian independence. Half a century later, Dr. Martin Luther King, Jr., used it as the handbook of the American civil rights movement. "As a result of Thoreau's writing and personal witness," he said, "we are the heirs of a legacy of creative protest." In 1962 the Reverend Trevor Bush, fighting apartheid in South Africa, noted, "Thoreau's influence in South Africa has been extremely important in our struggle to win rights for the oppressed nonwhite population of our country." "Civil Disobedience" was considered so subversive in America during the 1950s Communist witch-hunts that head Commie hunter Senator Joe McCarthy had the essay pulled from libraries.

SUMMARY

🕰 Celebrated the divinity of the individual, the sanctity of nature, the importance of intuition over reason.

🕰 Can get you through a really bad hair day, if not a roommate or spouse from the dark side.

🕰 Penned a blueprint for living an honorable, authentic life in *Walden.*

🕰 Share equal credit for that cheap strain of American optimism that gave us "Have a Nice Day" and smiley face buttons.

Nathaniel Hawthorne, 1804-1864, on a bad hair day

CHAPTER 4

NATHANIEL HAWTHORNE
(1804–1864)

A

YOU MUST REMEMBER THIS

Obsessed with sin and guilt, Hawthorne was the first great writer in the American tradition of psychological, subjective fiction.

MOST FAMOUS FOR

Doing for adultery what Melville did for the whale. *The Scarlet Letter* (1850) put the man on the map, but his short stories are also winners. You might want to peruse the following stories and novels:

- ★ *Twice-Told Tales* (1837)
- ★ *Mosses from an Old Manse* (1846)
- ★ *The House of the Seven Gables* (1851)
- ★ *The Blithedale Romance* (1852)
- ★ *Tanglewood Tales* (1853)
- ★ *The Marble Faun* (1860)

NATE THE GREAT

Fellow novelist Henry James once described Nathaniel Hawthorne at a dinner party of literary people in New York as looking like "a rogue who suddenly finds himself in a company of detectives." Henry may have been a good host, but even he couldn't have made Hawthorne comfortable with strangers. Perhaps Hawthorne's uneasiness came from his family, which had more skeletons than suits in their closets.

Hawthorne's first American ancestor, William Hathorne, was a magistrate who once had a Quaker woman publicly whipped in the streets. William's son, John Hathorne, inherited the family's kindly touch. As the (in)famous "Hanging Judge" of Salem, he presided over the 1692 witchcraft trials, during which a defendant cursed another of the three judges with the cry "God will give you blood to drink!" Small wonder Hawthorne added the *w* to the family name.

Hawthorne's childhood was no picnic, either. Hawthorne's father, a sea captain, died when his son was four, and the family lived in genteel poverty. After graduating from Bowdoin College in Maine in 1825, Hawthorne went home to Salem to become a writer. He served twelve years hard time in his bedroom learning to write. In 1828 he published his first work, *Fanshawe*, at his own expense. The book did badly. It was not until the publication of *Twice-Told Tales* in 1837 that he made a dent in the literary world.

A year later he fell hard for Sophia Peabody, a twenty-nine-year-old invalid neighbor, and took a job in the Boston Custom House to show his determination to win

SOMETHING WICKED
THIS WAY COMES

In 1692 witchcraft hysteria swept through Massachusetts like a bad case of shingles. Before the madness
ended, nineteen people and three dogs were hanged for
witchcraft. One man was pressed to death for refusing
to answer the indictment; fifty-five people openly con-
fessed to witchcraft. The insanity started when several
girls fell into seizures. The minister's niece accused the
family's black slave, Tituba, and two other outsiders of
bewitching them. Tituba was tortured into "confessing," and the girls began naming names. In 1953, in
The Crucible, playwright Arthur Miller used the madness
as an analogy for Senator Joe McCarthy's Communist
witch-hunts.

Salem Witchcraft Trials,
a hot time in the old town tonight

her hand. After a brief stay at the Brook Farm commune, he married Sophia and moved to Concord. The marriage was idyllic, and his political appointment as surveyor of the port of Salem in 1846—a tidy little sinecure—sealed his happiness. No wonder, then, that Hawthorne threw a hissy fit when the new political administration threw him out of office in 1849. *The Scarlet Letter* was his sensational revenge, and Hawthorne quickly wrote some of his greatest work, including *The House of the Seven Gables* and *The Blithedale Romance*. Despite his fame, Hawthorne still couldn't give up his day job; when old buddy Franklin Pierce, who had Peter Principled his way to the presidency, offered the American consulship in England, Hawthorne jumped.

Franklin Pierce, 1804-1869, 14th president of the United States and a charter member of the association of lesser presidents

The family returned to America in 1860, and Hawthorne set about plundering his journals for a new novel. But his strength was broken and nothing jelled. He died of a heart attack in 1864 while on a walking tour of New Hampshire.

LOOKING FOR LOVE
IN ALL THE WRONG PLACES

The novel is prefaced with "The Custom House," a remarkably tedious essay that claims to explain how Hawthorne found "a rag of scarlet cloth" shaped in the letter A in the Salem Custom House. It also explains how Hawthorne came by information about Hester Prynne, a Puritan forced to wear a scarlet A for "adultery." The information about the A is as fictitious as Hester Prynne, although history does record that several Puritans shtupped on the sly. Aside from setting the scene, "The Custom House" is sour grapes raised to art, in which Hawthorne explains how he lost his cozy sinecure when the new Whig administration threw out all the Democrats—including him. Along the way, he savages colleagues who kept their jobs. Nate was no fool; the satire of Salem was so vitriolic that the neighbors pulled in their welcome mats. The family moved to Concord. Still, revenge is sweet.

WHO'S WHO ☞

The Scarlet Letter:

A LITERARY TOUT SHEET

Hester Prynne: The proud, regal beauty who stands by her man and learns that love doesn't conquer all.

Roger Chillingworth: Hester's chilly burger of a husband, who manages to wrest defeat from the jaws of victory.

The Reverend Arthur Dimmesdale: Hester's wimpy lover. Is this the best you can do, girl?

Pearl: The product of Hester's two-step with Arthur; poster child for *not* sparing the rod.

As the story opens, a gaggle of gossips are standing outside the Boston jail jeering Hester Prynne, who has been convicted of the crime of adultery. The townspeo-

THE PURITANS

The Puritans were English Protestants who sought to "purify" the Church of England by removing all religious doodads. When the Church refused to be purified, the sore losers packed up and headed for the New World. There they were free to persecute their neighbors and preach predestination, the belief that all humans are unworthy sinners, except for the "elect," those destined from birth for God's grace and salvation. How can you tell who's on the A team? There's the rub. The trick is to act as if you've made the cut so you fool the neighbors and maybe even the Big Guy upstairs.

Puritans come to America,
giving "coach" a whole new meaning

ple are furious that the court had been merciful toward Hester; instead of the promised public hanging, she has been condemned to wear a scarlet A on her chest and serve a little hard time. Today she and her infant (proof of her sin) are forced to stand on the scaffold in shame. The suspicion is that Hester has been spared death only through the intercession of her minister, the Reverend Arthur Dimmesdale. Hester has refused to name her partner in pleasure, much to Dimmesdale's relief. On the edge of the crowd, there is an elderly, deformed man whom Hester recognizes—her husband! Two years earlier he had sent her alone to America, and she has never seen or heard from him until this moment.

Later, when Hester refuses to reveal her lover's name to her husband, he vows revenge. He takes the name "Roger Chillingworth" to conceal his identity and swears Hester to secrecy. Hester and her daughter, Pearl, move to an isolated part of the village, where Hester makes her living sewing. Pearl is such an imp that the church decides Hester is an unfit mother. Dimmesdale again saves the day with a heartfelt appeal on Hester's behalf. Suspicious of Dimmesdale's motives, Chillingworth clings to him like the high-priced plastic wrap. Shocked at Dimmesdale's rapid mental and physical decline, Hester reveals Chillingworth's true identity to Dimmesdale. The lovers make plans to leave the 'hood for the Old World, but Chillingworth books passage on the same boat.

Before the boat sails, Dimmesdale makes the greatest speech of his career, but he looks like something the cat refused to drag in. He calls Hester and Pearl to the scaffold with him, admits his guilt, tears aside his vestment, and falls down dead. Some people say that there was a scarlet A burned into his chest; others swear that his chest was smooth and unscarred. Chillingworth, deprived of his raison d'être, dies within a year. Hester and Pearl disappear, but years later Hester returns alone. It is thought that Pearl has married and moved to England. Hester places the scarlet letter back on her chest and

Hester Pryne, Hawthorne's most famous literary creation

lives quietly in her cottage. Once a sign of shame, the letter has become a symbol of mercy because of Hester's great kindness and good deeds. At her death Hester is buried beside Dimmesdale, their tombstone engraved with an A.

A'S NOT FOR APPLE IN THIS TOWN

A creative people, the Puritans had letters to punish almost every crime. Those under the influence got to stand in the town square with a large red D for "drunk" around their necks, while thieves were decorated with a T. A man who "attempted lewdness with diverse women" was severely whipped and sentenced to wear a V for "uncleanness" (V and U were interchangeable). People who took the Lord's name in vain wore a B for "blasphemy." But every now and again tragedy struck—two crimes with the same letter! For example, since I was already taken for "incest," the Puritans were forced to improvise when some of their own dallied with an Indian: they wore a cutout of an Indian on their arm for a year. Wearing a letter was the preferred punishment; adulterers, for example, were more often branded, mutilated, or hanged than decorated.

YOU PLAY, YOU PAY

The Scarlet Letter was Hawthorne's first great success, praised for its "subtle knowledge of character" and "tragic power." Henry James called the novel "the finest piece of imaginative writing yet put forth in America."

The novel focuses on sin and guilt and their effect

on individuals and society. For those of you who haven't tried the Deadly Sins on for size, sinning isn't as simple as it seems: you have sins of passion and those of principle. Dimmesdale understands the difference: "We are not, Hester, the worst sinners in the world. There is one worse than even the polluted priest! That old man's revenge has been blacker than my sin. He has violated, in cold blood, the sanctity of the human heart." Chillingworth is the true criminal because he has boldly gone where no one belongs—and he violates the soul.

Hester, whose sin is revealed, grows through her suffering, comes to term with her sin, and reconciles herself with God. In contrast, Dimmesdale is tortured by secret guilt and cannot make peace with himself or with God. His guilt manifests itself physically, and it kills him.

Hawthorne's obsession with the mysteries of the human heart places him in the middle of the Romantic tradition, which valued imagination, freedom, emotion, wildness, the rights of the individual, the nobility of the common person, and the appeal of pastoral life. But Hawthorne was too concerned with the Puritan past to adopt the optimistic vision of Emerson, Thoreau (see page XX, "The Transcendentalists"), Irving, and Cooper. Hawthorne is allied instead with Melville and Poe, and thus is part of the "dark Romantic" category.

12 RM HANDYMAN'S SPECIAL; NEEDS TLC

The House of the Seven Gables, once the object of the

local realtor's lust, is now a candidate for urban renewal. Its current occupant, old Hepzibah Pyncheon, is also in need of major renovation. Hepzibah, among the last of the Pyncheons, lacks both her ancestors' money and their chutzpah. Colonel Pyncheon, the man who built the house 160 years ago, swindled the land from Matthew Maule by charging him with witchcraft. A feisty chap, Maule cursed the Pyncheons from the gallows, screaming, "God will give ye blood to drink!" During the housewarming Colonel Pyncheon was found dead in his chair, his shirtfront covered in blood. Time to shut yourself in the room and push the bureau across the door.

Just before his death, Colonel Pyncheon was arranging to buy a chunk of Maine. Naturally, none of the heirs has ever been able to find the deed and claim the legacy. They do get Maule's Curse, however, free of charge.

The Old Manse, home of Emerson and later, Hawthorne

The cupboard as empty as her life, Hepzibah sets aside what remains of her tattered pride and opens up a small shop to sell candy, needles, and other necessities. Pre-

WHO'S
WHO
☛

The House of the Seven Gables:
A LITERARY TOUT SHEET

Colonel Pyncheon: Go ahead, make his day: the Donald (Trump, not Duck) of the Puritan set.

Hepzibah Pyncheon: The prototype for old maids; she'd never make it on "The Golden Girls."

Clifford Pyncheon: The lamp is lit but nobody's home, that is, he is none too smart. But after thirty years in prison, a man's entitled to a little latitude.

Holgrave: Hawthorne's alter ego: a sensitive yet manly man who has seen and done it all. Objectively speaking, the man is hot.

Phoebe Pyncheon: The sweet young thing, a downtown girl with uptown class.

Judge Jaffrey Pyncheon: As vicious as a mink, a monster who hides his avarice behind a façade of philanthropy.

The House of the Seven Gables: The Bates Mansion. Mama's missing, but who notices?

dictably, Hepzibah botches the small business, but the arrival of her perky young cousin, Phoebe Pyncheon, saves the day. Phoebe's charm, youth, and common sense lighten up the gloomy mansion and Hepzibah's life. Soon after, Hepzibah's dotty brother, Clifford, comes home from a thirty-year stay in jail. One sandwich shy of a picnic, Clifford tries to jump out of a window to join a passing parade and is generally a handful for Phoebe and Hepzibah.

Judge Jaffrey Pyncheon, a nasty piece of work, visits Hepzibah and demands to see Clifford, who he thinks has the deed to the tract of land in Maine. Well aware that Clifford's hold on reality is tenuous at best, Hepzibah refuses to arrange the meeting, but Jaffrey threatens to have Clifford committed to the insane asylum unless he agrees to his demands. Cowed, Hepzibah searches around town for Clifford, only to find upon her return that Jaffrey has choked to death on his own blood. Terrified that they will be blamed for the death, Hepzibah and Clifford hop the first train out of town. Holgrave, the house border, finds Jaffrey's body. He breaks the news to Phoebe when she returns from the country, slipping in his declaration of love for her. Not surprisingly, she returns his affections. Meanwhile, Clifford and Hepzibah come home, having realized that you can run but you can't hide.

The judge rules that Jaffrey died a natural death, and that Jaffrey framed Clifford for Colonel Pyncheon's death. The surviving Pyncheons inherit Jaffrey's lush country estate. Holgrave reveals that his name is really Maule, descendant of the cursing Maules, and produces what proves to be a worthless deed to the land in Maine. Phoebe and Holgrave plan their nuptials, and everyone lives happily ever after.

BIOLOGY IS DESTINY

Sin redux. Hawthorne states the moral outright in the Preface: "The wrong-doing of one generation lives into the successive ones, and, divesting itself of every temporary advantage, becomes a pure and uncontrollable mischief." The ending, however, reveals that all is not lost, for some people have enough strength of will to reject a "dark necessity" to live happily ever after.

What makes this a real thriller-chiller are the Gothic gloom and doom and the blood and guts. There's also a crumbling mansion, an ancient curse, and visits from the spirit world. In short, everything you love in Freddy Krueger but without the popcorn.

THE NOT-SO-YOUNG AND RESTLESS

Miles Coverdale, a mediocre poet, journeys a short distance from his comfortable quarters in town to participate with other quasi-reformers in the Blithedale experiment in communal living. He is joined by the sensual, hothouse-flower-adorned Zenobia, a well-known feminist writer and femme fatale. Along for the ride is Hollingsworth, a zealous philanthropist and reformer who wants Zenobia's bucks rather than her body so that he can

WHO'S
H
O
☞

The Blithedale Romance:
A LITERARY TOUT SHEET

Miles Coverdale: What *is* Miles covering? The mysterious all-knowing narrator.

Zenobia: Mama's so hot she's steaming.

Priscilla Moodie: Mousey gets it all in the end.

Hollingsworth: A cross between a buffalo and a moose, determined to reform the criminal element.

Westervelt: Seriously smarmy, down to the shoddy dental work.

Old Moodie: The father of them all.

turn Blithedale into a home for reformed convicts. The pale Priscilla, former seamstress and current pursemaker, enters the picture and feels an instant (and one-sided) bond with Zenobia.

Old Moodie drops by to ask about Priscilla and Zenobia, but Coverdale can't figure out their relationship. Then it's the mysterious Professor Westervelt's turn to ask about the ladies. When the smoke clears, we learn that Old Moodie, now destitute but formerly rich and indolent, fathered Zenobia by his first marriage, Priscilla by his second. Naturally, neither girl knows about the other, so Moodie visits Zenobia to command her to take

*"Roger hasn't figured it out yet. I guess
he never read* The Scarlet Letter *after all."*

BROOK FARM

Hawthorne based *The Blithedale Romance* on the real
Brook Farm, the most famous commune of the nineteenth century, an era that witnessed no fewer than
fifty different experiments in communal life. Located in
Roxbury, Massachusetts, about nine miles from Boston,
Brook Farm endured six years, from 1841 to 1847. It
began as an attempt to live the Transcendental life,
close to nature. Although not a Transcendentalist himself, Hawthorne did live at Brook Farm from April until
November 1841 and owned stock in the place. Other
noteworthy residents included newspaper editor Charles
Ellery Dana, minister and educator William Henry Channing, minister and reformer Theodore Parker, and minister George Ripley.

care of Priscilla, weaned on tales of her mythical big sis. Zenobia and the mysterious gold-banded Westervelt use Priscilla as the Veiled Lady and experiment with mesmerism. Hollingsworth, that virile though thinly drawn bear of a man, chooses Priscilla over Zenobia. Zenobia, unable to accept that she's been ditched for the little sister, promptly drowns herself in the river. The gang fish out the body, bury it, and everyone drifts off. Hollingsworth and Prissy (who now has all the money) marry, but his great plans are never realized: he sees himself as Zenobia's murderer and thus will waste his life. After the funeral Coverdale leaves Blithedale, but not before revealing to his Gentle Readers that he, too, has loved Priscilla.

BLITHEDEAL

With such rich pickings as *The Scarlet Letter* and *The House of the Seven Gables, The Blithedale Romance* was often dismissed as "the slightest and most colorless" of Hawthorne's novels. In the 1950s, however, the novel came into its own; by the time of the commune mania of the 1970s, it was hot stuff.

The novel is generally seen as a story about Coverdale, who travels to Blithedale to find a purpose in life. The narration chronicles the failure of his inner exploration and his terrible isolation. He escapes Chillingworth's fate only because the book is a romance rather than a tragedy.

Just as the Puritans' religious fanaticism and isolation could not save them from human nature, so Brook Farm cannot offer a haven for the passions that provoke countless Amy Fishers and Joey Buttafuocos. The love triangle in the book reaches a climax because the players are thrown together; instead of a refuge, Brook Farm becomes an arena for love's tragedy.

SUMMARY

⏱ Raised guilt to an art form. His "allegories of the heart" show people torn between the tragic evil of human nature and a human sympathy for man's natural passions.

⏱ Also tried to corner the market on sin, including the consequences of pride, selfishness, and hidden guilt.

⏱ Did romance as well as the Colonel does chicken. Remember that Hawthorne claims romance is a work of fiction that "claims a certain latitude with the ordinary course of human experience," as long as it shows "the truth of the human heart."

⏱ Showed keen psychological insights that paved the way for Melville and Faulkner.

Edgar Allan Poe (1809–1849)

CHAPTER 5

EDGAR ALLAN POE

(1809–1849)

YOU MUST REMEMBER THIS

Even though Poe married jail bait and ingested every controlled substance short of plutonium, he created the modern short story and the detective story, and wrote some nifty poetry.

MOST FAMOUS FOR

Substance abuse, but here's the best work anyway:

Poems
★ "Lenore" (1831)
★ "The Raven" (1845)
★ "Ulalume" (1847)
★ "Annabel Lee" (1849)

Short Stories
★ "Ligeia" (1838)
★ *The Narrative of Arthur Gordon Pym* (1838)
★ "The Fall of the House of Usher" (1839)
★ "The Masque of the Red Death" (1842)
★ "The Pit and the Pendulum" (1843)
★ "The Gold Bug" (1843)
★ "The Tell-Tale Heart" (1843)
★ "The Purloined Letter" (1845)
★ "The Cask of Amontillado" (1846)

NOTHING A LITTLE PROZAC AND A POLO MALLET WOULDN'T CURE

Poe was born to two struggling actors who lived in a Boston apartment so small it's no wonder he stuck to short stories. It was not an auspicious beginning: his mother was dying of tuberculosis; his father, of alcoholism. Left an orphan within three years, the toddler was adopted by John and Frances Allan, prosperous merchants in Richmond, Virginia.

Frances immediately bonded with the young boy, but John kept his distance. Nonetheless, John gave Edgar the finest education, both at home and abroad. Edgar excelled in sports as well as academics; although he was cruelly taunted for his lowly parentage, he made a number of close friends.

When he was seventeen, Poe enrolled in the University of Virginia. UVA was a happening kind of place, and within the day of his arrival, Poe managed to gamble away his entire term's allowance. By the end of the term, he owed more than $2,500. What skill he lacked with cards he more than made up with in drink, managing to stay drunk most of the term. Astonishingly, he also aced his studies, earning the highest distinction. Unimpressed with Edgar's academic accomplishments, John Allan yanked his drunken card sharp from school faster than you could say "Deal 'em out and pour me a stiff one." Soon after, Edgar hit the road, heading for Bean Town. Boston was then the center of publishing, and Edgar was determined to write the Great American Something. At his own expense, Poe published *Tamerlane and Other Poems*. Only fifty copies were printed, few sold, and they made nary a ripple in the literary pond. In desperation, Poe enlisted in the Army. He was eighteen years old.

Although he did well soldiering, Poe soon realized that he was not cut from khaki cloth. Logic decreed resigning; instead, Poe decided to enter West Point, again manifesting an ability to shoot himself in the foot, figuratively speaking. He entered the U.S. Military Academy in July of 1830, and by midterms knew that he was in the wrong place. After getting himself court-martialed, Poe traveled to New York, where he managed to get a book of poems published. Like his previous attempt, this volume vanished more thoroughly than Jimmy Hoffa. On to Baltimore.

After months of living in a style to which no one would like to become accustomed, Poe won $50 and some recognition for his short stories. He also fell in love with his preteen cousin, Virginia. She embodied his ideal: pale, dark-haired, vacant (and proud of it). In 1835, when Poe was twenty-six, he married Virginia, who had finally turned thirteen. In the meantime, John Allan had died, cutting Poe out of his will completely. For the rest of his life, the family (now including Virginia's mother, Poe's aunt) trekked back and forth between New York, Philadelphia, Baltimore, and Richmond, surviving mainly on bread and molasses, as Poe tried to carve out a career. His astonishing talent secured him a number of editing jobs; his equally astonishing capacity for drink got him fired from them all. During a trip to see President Tyler, he was reported to be so drunk that he wore his coat inside out. History does not record if the President noticed.

That he managed to write anything at all is amazing; that he wrote so much of value is nothing short of remarkable. Virginia's death from tuberculosis in 1847 sent him reeling, if anyone could tell. Two years later he decided to hop on the wagon; he fell right off with a tremendous crash, landing in a tavern. He died three days later. "This death was a suicide," French poet Charles Baudelaire remarked, "a suicide prepared for a long time."

With enviable skill, Poe managed to screw up his life even from beyond the grave. The man he had appointed as his literary executor, Rufus Griswold, wrote a slanderous obit, claiming that Poe had been expelled from college, committed plagiarism, and drank himself to death. And that was the nice part.

To the hoi polloi, Poe's fame rests on the whiz-bang virtuosity of such poems as "The Raven," "Ulalume," and "The Bells" and on his receiving line of sociopaths,

Edgar Allan Poe Museum, Philadelphia

necrophiliacs, and assorted deviants. Lit crit types celebrate his criticism (the bulk of his writing) including the slash-and-burn reviews and the philosophies of composition.

CHARLES BAUDELAIRE (1821–1867)

Charles Baudelaire, 1821-1867, French poet

Wild and crazy Baudelaire catapulted to literary prominence in 1848 with his French translations of Poe's writings. His major work, a book of poems called *Les Fleurs de mal (The Flowers of Evil)*, appeared in 1857 and got him slapped with a morals charge. *Les Paradis artificiels* (1860) did little to endear him to the general public; he died soon after. His poems tend to appeal to skinny men and women who dress in black, drink absinthe, obsess over death, and smoke incessantly.

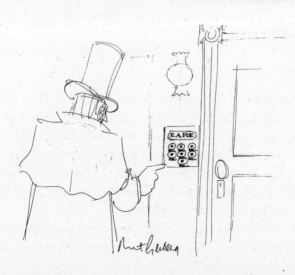

"THE RAVEN"

Once upon a midnight dreary, while I pondered,
weak and weary,
Over many a quaint and curious volume of
forgotten lore—
While I nodded, nearly napping, suddenly there
came a tapping,
As of some one gently rapping, rapping at my
chamber door.
" 'Tis some visitor," I muttered, "tapping at my
chamber door—
Only this, and nothing more."

Ah, distinctly I remember it was in the bleak December;
And each separate dying ember wrought its ghost
upon the floor.
Eagerly I wished the morrow;—vainly I had sought
to borrow
From my books surcease of sorrow—sorrow for the
lost Lenore—
For the rare and radiant maiden whom the angels
named Lenore—
Nameless *here* for evermore.

"The Raven" is a ballad of eighteen six-line stanzas
that's about as subtle as The Donald. It describes the
nightmarish story of a young man, mourning the death
of his beloved Lenore, driven mad by a raven. The bird
is no Joan Rivers—all it can say is "Nevermore"—so we
know the narrator has a dicey grip on reality to start
with. Bet you're really surprised.

The first seven stanzas describe the spook-house setting and the narrator's need for Valium. In stanzas eight

Edgar Allan Poe supplements his
writing income moonlighting as
a Boston weatherman

*"Out here we're calling for a midnight dreary and
down here we'll be deep into darkness peering."*

through eleven, the narrator chats up the bird, but all
it says is "Nevermore." Even though the word has no
relevance to any discoverable meaning, the narrator is
unnerved. In stanzas twelve and thirteen, the narrator
treats the bird like a feathered Ouija board, peppering
it with questions. As his frenzy mounts, the narrator asks
the bird if he will ever be reunited with his beloved Lenore. The raven's answer is predictable. The narrator
then demands that the bird leave; the bird hunkers
down for the long haul, and narrator goes round the
bend.

A raven, a member of the crow family. The largest of all songbirds, known for its intelligence, sociability, and role in legend and folklore. Also noted for its large vocabulary

"The Raven" is Poe's most famous poem, not only because parents mangle parts of it to remind their offspring that they once knew poetry, but also because Poe immortalized its creation in an essay entitled "The Philosophy of Composition." The essay explores how the poem's dramatic elements are underscored by the stanzas' maddening rhythms and rhymes. The dramatic juxtaposition of the black bird perched on the white bust, central to the play of light and shadow, helps the poem build to its frenzied climax, the speaker's overwhelming sorrow and insane desperation. The poem objectifies Poe's belief that the beauty of a poem is an end in itself. Good thing, too: hate to have to look for Deep Meaning in this baby. Poe attacked what he called the "epic mania" (a poem had to be long to be good) and the "didactic heresy" (a poem had to teach a lesson) and created a (firsthand?) view of insanity.

"ANNABEL LEE"

It was many and many a year ago,
    In a kingdom by the sea
That a maiden there lived whom you may know
    By the name of ANNABEL LEE;
And this maiden she lived with no other thought
    Than to love and be loved by me.

I was a child and *she* was a child,
    In this kingdom by the sea,
But we loved with a love that was more than love—
    I and my ANNABEL LEE—
With a love that the winged seraphs of heaven
    Coveted her and me.

The rest of the ballad tells Poe's usual story—boy loves girl, girl dies, boy spends every night in her tomb lying next to her dead body. Keep in mind this girl's been dead for *years*. The poem is either an admirable testament to everlasting love or the maniacal ravings of a psychopath. Do we admire the speaker as a devoted lover or lock him up as a stalker? Consider Poe's work as a whole . . . then throw away the key.

"Annabel Lee" is famous for its haunting rhythms and lulling repetition. The rhymes capture a wave-like cadence; the repetition of "sea," "Lee," and "me" especially call for a hit of No Doz. Lines such as "But we loved with a love that was more than love" are almost numbing; the out-of-body dreamy feeling is reinforced by gliding consonants such as *m, n, l,* and *s.*

"LENORE"

"Lenore" is an elegy, a lament for the death of the young and beautiful Lenore. The twenty-six lines contrast the sincere grief of Guy De Vere, Lenore's fiancé, and the false sentiments of her friends and family. Actually, no one is really sure what the darned thing is about, or even how many people are speaking. All anyone can agree on is that this poem—like many of Poe's verses— is about the death of a young woman, his favorite topic. Whatever its meaning, the haunting rhythms echo with great beauty.

The unnamed narrator marries the beautiful and brilliant Ligeia, and they live happily in Germany until she dies of a mysterious illness. Then he marries the equally beautiful but not as brilliant Rowena, and they live together miserably in a decaying English abbey. Rowena suffers bouts of illness; the narrator pines for his lost Ligeia. The narrator becomes addicted to opium, and in his drug-induced dreams he cries out for Ligeia. Calling out in bed for a former wife does not do great things for a marriage, but Rowena has problems of her own: she thinks the walls have eyes—and maybe ears and limbs as well.

One night when Rowena is more agitated than usual, the narrator walks across the room to get her some wine. As he pours the drink, he hears footsteps and sees a few drops of ruby-colored liquid fall into the goblet from an invisible source. Soon after, Rowena dies. As he holds vigil by her shrouded corpse, the narrator notices that she appears to have come back to life. After a terrifying struggle, she dies again—but not before the narrator has a vision of Ligeia. This

WHO'S WHO

"Ligeia":
A LITERARY TOUT SHEET

The Narrator: A marrying kind of guy.

Ligeia: You can't keep a good lady down; Wife No. 1.

Lady Rowena Trevanion: Wife No. 2.

occurs a few times, until the narrator is ready for the men with butterfly nets and we're ready to whack Rowena upside her undead head.

At dawn the shrouded corpse rises from the bed and unwraps the cloth to reveal—"the full, and the black, and the wild eyes—of my lost love—of the lady—of the LADY LIGEIA." You were expecting maybe Mel Brooks?

The eponymous heroine of Ligeia,
Poe's brilliant tale of fantasy and terror

INVASION OF THE BODY SNATCHER

Toto, we're definitely not in Kansas anymore. Poe called "Ligeia" his best tale, and with cause: it's a brilliant ride of terror and fantasy, a real white-knuckle flight. Poe classified the story as an "arabesque," a tale that has no credibility in reality yet is nonetheless told seriously, without the tone of satiric mockery he used in the fantastic tales he called "grotesques." In its terror, "Ligeia" is akin to "The Fall of the House of Usher," "The Cask of Amontillado," and "The Tell-Tale Heart." The theme is a familiar one in Poe: psychic survival through reincarnation, an invasion of the body snatcher.

More than anyone else, Poe is responsible for the emergence of the short story as a respected and popular genre. He was the first to define the short story, arguing that it deserves the respect given to its big bro, the novel. His definition, which first appeared in a review of Hawthorne's *Twice-Told Tales*, asserts that the short story should achieve "a certain unique or single effect." To do so, every incident, character, and detail must mesh. "In the whole composition there should be no word written, of which the tendency, direct or indirect, is not to the one preestablished design."

"Ligeia" has provided considerable grist for academic mills. Some critics argue that the title character is not really a woman at all, but rather "the incarnation of German idealism"; others, that she is a witch or a "revenant," a spirit who keeps returning to earth. As for the narrator, some see him as a murderer who poisoned Rowena with tainted wine, others as a victim of circumstance. The most intriguing question concerns Ligeia's "return." Does she really come back from the other side, or is the final vision a drug-induced hallucination? However you read this tale, it's a humdinger.

HERE'S JOHNNY!

We have the Gothic tradition to thank for such gems as *Sorority Girl Slashers at the Bowl-a-Rama* and *Abbott and Costello Meet the Bride of Frankenstein*. First popular in the late eighteenth century and the early nineteenth, Gothic lit emphasized mystery, horror, violence, terror, decapitations, undead dead, premature entombment, spooky castles, rattling chains, and sometimes even a little perverted sex. Long before Stephen King, the trendsetters were Horace Walpole (*The Castle of Otranto*, 1764), Clara Reeve (*The Champion of Virtue*, 1777), Ann Radcliffe (*The Mysteries of Udolpho*, 1794), and Mary Wollstonecraft Shelley (*Frankenstein*, 1818).

"THE GOLD BUG"

While looking around Sullivan's Island for entomological specimens, William Legrand finds an entirely new insect, a gold bug. On the way home, Legrand draws a picture of the bug for his friend, the narrator, to examine. When the friend mocks the drawing as resembling a skull, Legrand takes another look, pales, and shoves the sketch into his wallet. A month later Jupiter visits the narrator to report that Legrand is crazy.

The friend returns to the island and dutifully follows Legrand and the gold bug around the island. At this point the gold bug appears saner than Legrand. Things don't get any better when Legrand suddenly orders Jupiter to climb a giant tulip tree. On the outer edge of the tree, he finds a human skull. On Legrand's orders, he drops the bug through the left eye socket of the skull. After completing a series of feverish measurements, Legrand digs in search of buried treasure. Nothing. Jupiter admits he

WHO'S WHO
☞

"The Gold Bug":
A LITERARY TOUT SHEET

The Narrator: Well, someone has to tell the story.

William Legrand: Something rare in Poe: a sane person.

Jupiter: Legrand's servant. Good help is *so* hard to find.

mistakenly dropped the bug through the *right* eye. Remeasure, redig, and violà! a chest of legendary treasure.

Legrand explains how he solved the mystery, found the treasure, and lived happily ever after, even without his Captain Crunch magic decoder ring. When the paper on which he had drawn the bug was exposed to fire, the skull emerged. He dipped the paper into water, revealing a series of numbers. Got all that? Or are you one of those people who skips ahead to the last page?

"The Gold Bug," Poe's most famous short story

DICK LIT

The general lack of unpleasantness in this story is quite unnerving. No living entombments, screaming maniacs, bloody limbs—not even a decaying mansion. Was Poe finally getting the right medication? Nope: he was inventing a whole new genre, the detective story. He was thirty-four years old.

"The Gold Bug," Poe's most famous story, belongs to a small group of stories he called "tales of ratiocination," stories in which logic is used to solve a mystery. Among these tales are "The Murders in the Rue Morgue," "The Mystery of Marie Rogêt," and "The Purloined Letter"—in which amateur detective Monsieur C. Auguste Dupin unravels a puzzle. Arthur Conan Doyle's Sherlock Holmes stories were inspired by the Dupin tales.

Aside from the fact that you can read these stories when you're alone at night, the tone and structure are also different from Poe's horror tales. The language is unemotional, analytical, and rational. His horror tales build to a violent climax, usually involving an ax in someone's skull. In Poe's detective tales, the action takes place in the first half of the story; most of the latter half is devoted to solving the mystery set up earlier. If you want to be a nitpicker, Poe had some problems with geography and topography in "The Gold Bug" and the humor falls flatter than Kansas, but the mystery is wonderfully suspenseful.

Admiring Poe is "the mark of a decidedly primitive stage of reflection," Henry James sniffed; T. S. Eliot said that Poe's mind was that of "a highly gifted young person before puberty." Yet the French Symbolists worshiped him: Charles Baudelaire and Stéphane Mallarmé placed Poe right up there with fine wine and smelly cheese. Several British writers who oddly enough all went by three names (as did Poe) were all big fans—Dante Gabriel Rossetti, Robert Louis Stevenson, Arthur Conan Doyle, George Bernard Shaw—climbed aboard the bandwagon of praise as well. Poe's influence is clearly seen in the work of American writers like Edwin Arlington Robinson, Frank Norris, Theodore Dreiser, and William

ELEMENTARY, MY DEAR WATSON

Whodunits caught on big in 1887, when Sir Arthur Conan Doyle published *A Study in Scarlet*, introducing Sherlock Holmes, the most famous detective—real or fictional—of all time. Within five years Holmes, the arch-fiend Professor Moriarty, and the terminally dense narrator, Dr. Watson, were so successful that Doyle was able to forsake his medical practice for fiction, penning four novelettes and fifty-six short stories about Holmes, among the most famous being *The Sign of the Four* (1890) and *The Hound of the Baskervilles* (1902). Like

Trekkies, Holmes groupies flourish, the most famous group being the Baker Street Irregulars.

Sir Arthur Conan Doyle, 1859-1930; British physician and detective writer, creator of master sleuth Sherlock Holmes

Faulkner. Besides, he's made work for countless graduate students and scholars, who while away their worthless lives arguing whether Poe was a pioneering writer or merely a morose windbag.

WHODUNITS

Doyle may have been the first to join Poe's parade, but he was far from the last. As with designer water, we soon got specialized detectives. G. K. Chesterton (1874–1936) created the priest-detective Father Brown; Agatha Christie (1891–1976), the Belgian Hercule Poirot. Earl Derr Biggers (1884–1933) went ethnic in a big way with Charlie Chan, Rex Stout (1886–1975) hit the food circuit with gourmet detective Nero Wolfe, and Dorothy Sayers (1893–1957) went upscale with Lord Peter Wimsey. Erle Stanley Gardner (1889–1970) invented Perry Mason, eventually opening up a whole new career for portly Raymond Burr. Dashiell Hammett (1894–1961) and Raymond Chandler (1888–1959) took the hard-boiled route with Sam Spade and Philip Marlowe, respectively.

SUMMARY

⏱ Created the detective story.

⏱ Invented the psychotic-murder story and paved the way for such pop-culture icons as Mama Bates of *Psycho* fame, Freddy Krueger, and PMS cheerleaders with chainsaws.

⏱ Set up the rules for the short story.

⏱ Crafted memorable poetry about dead lovers and large black birds.

Harriet Beecher Stowe, 1811-1896,
writer and abolitionist

CHAPTER 6

HARRIET BEECHER STOWE

(1811–1896)

YOU MUST REMEMBER THIS

Abraham Lincoln called Stowe "the little woman who started this great big war." *Uncle Tom's Cabin*, Stowe's antislavery tract, was the most influential book of the nineteenth century. Stowe was the most famous American woman of her day.

MOST FAMOUS FOR

Her courageous stand against injustice, discrimination, and oppression. The Hillary Rodham Clinton of the religious set, Stowe was most famous for the following novels:

- ★ *Uncle Tom's Cabin* (1852)
- ★ *Dred: A Tale of the Great Dismal Swamp* (1856)
- ★ *The Pearl of Orr's Island* (1862)
- ★ *Oldtown Folks* (1869)
- ★ *Lady Byron Vindicated* (1870)

SAINTS, SINNERS, AND BEECHERS

A ll eleven Beecher kids had moxie. No doubt most of it had rubbed off from Daddy, a charismatic up-and-comer in the hellfire-and-damnation school of preaching. When not sending people to hell for white bread sinning, Lyman Beecher attacked them for drinking (in a day when rum and opium was the childhood remedy of choice), dancing, and dueling. His sons were expected to study for the clergy; his daughters, to marry into it. Lyman recognized Harriet's brilliance early. "Hattie is a genius," he wrote. "I would give a hundred dollars if she was a boy."

Harriet arm-wrestled with religious doubts at a local Connecticut school until she was thirteen, when her elder sister Catherine started the Hartford Female Seminary. Catherine was about as gentle as a croquet mallet to the side of the head, and Harriet meekly toed the line as both pupil and teacher. In 1832 the family was uprooted when Lyman accepted the presidency of the Lane Theological Seminary in Cincinnati. "It's the Athens of the West," he crowed to his brood, while Harriet claimed, "I never saw a place so capable of being rendered a Paradise." "Porkopolis," the natives dubbed their city, paying backhanded homage to the slaughterhouses and meatpacking plants, but cleverly overlooking the frequent cholera epidemics—and the slaves right across the river.

Catherine opened another school, drafted her malleable sibling once again, leaving Harriet little time to learn to apply mascara. Fortunately, she soon met someone who appreciated her less visible qualities: Calvin Stowe, a pudgy preacher ten years her senior. In 1835 Harriet and Calvin fell so deeply in love that she was able to overlook his financial incompetence, gluttony, and hypochondria. Calvin soon proved that he was indeed unable to make money, but he sure could make children—seven, all told.

Calvin's $600 a year didn't begin to cover the bacon, so Harriet took over breadwinning along with her usual child care, cooking, cleaning, shopping, sewing, washing, and ironing. Publishers cheerfully paid $2 a page for her charming stories of New England life, and Harriet churned them out as fast as her homemade butter. But the horrors of slavery had eaten at her for years. Sud-

Cincinnati, Ohio, in the mid-19th century

TRAFFIC IN HUMAN FLESH

In 1444 Portugal became the first modern nation to meet its labor needs by importing blacks captured from Africa; Spain and England soon followed, the New World bringing up the rear in 1619. The development of the plantation system in America around 1650 codified the barbarity. In 1800 there were nearly a million black slaves in America; by 1860 the figure had quadrupled. Individuals and members of nearly all sects defended slavery. Although antislavery views grew steadily, many who supported abolition were unwilling to dispute what many citizens held to be their right to own slaves.

---

denly, the plot for her most famous novel appeared to her in a vision in church; her children sobbed when they read the first chapters. *Uncle Tom's Cabin* (1852) brought Stowe astonishing fame as well as an astonishing amount of money, which vanished quickly into the gaping maw of the Stowes' considerable brood.

Because she thought that few Northerners would believe her tale if she presented slavery at its cruelest, Stowe had set out to "show the *best side* of the thing, and something *faintly approaching the worst*." Shocked by charges that she had not presented a balanced portrayal of slavery, the following year she published *A Key to Uncle Tom's Cabin*, documented case histories to defend the novel. Her modesty unshaken by the enormous success of her novel, Stowe traveled widely and continued to write, publishing *Dred: A Tale of the Great Dismal Swamp* in 1856 and *The Pearl of Orr's Island* in 1860. Between 1863 and 1870, she churned out ten books for a quick buck, including children's stories, religious poetry, and biography.

In 1869 the scribe of the Lord once again felt herself summoned to take up her pen in a holy cause, this time defending Lady Byron against charges that she had wronged her hunky hubby, the British poet Lord Byron. All the principals were safely dead, but the issue was still steaming: Stowe was roundly reviled and even barred from the British Isles for defaming a national hero. The scandal eventually died down, and Stowe embarked on a series of wildly successful lecture tours before quietly succumbing to old age in her eighty-fifth year.

UNCLE TOM'S CABIN: THE MAN THAT WAS A THING

The novel opens on the Shelby plantation, a few years before the Civil War. Encumbered with debt, Shelby is forced to sell some of his slaves. Haley, the wily slave trader, picks Uncle Tom, Shelby's favorite and most loyal slave, and Harry, a handsome little boy. Eliza, Harry's mother, overhears the conversation, grabs her son, and flees. She tries to convince Uncle Tom to come with her, but he remains loyal to his "Mas'r."

With Haley in hot pursuit, Eliza escapes across the Ohio River by leaping across the ice floes. She and her boy are sheltered by Quakers, and Eliza is reunited with her husband, George, a slave who had escaped from a neighboring plantation. Soon the family is bound for Canada.

Uncle Tom is rewarded for his loyalty by being sold down the river. During the steamboat trip, he is be-friended by Eva St. Clare, a tot so angelic she could be Shirley Temple on Prozac. Before they reach port, Uncle

WHO'S WHO ☞

Uncle Tom's Cabin:
A LITERARY TOUT SHEET

A Cast of Thousands

Uncle Tom: The Christ figure who got a bum rap in his own day and in ours.

Simon Legree: The cruelest villain in American literature: a reputation he richly deserved.

Eva St. Clare: An impossibly angelic five-year-old; if a real child of yours ever acted this well, you'd start counting your Valiums.

Mr. St. Clare: A wealthy slaveowner who promises Tom his freedom but cashes in his chips before he can make good his word.

Mrs. St. Clare: Not this decade, dear: I just had my nails done and I have a crushing headache.

Eliza: A courageous slave whose fierce family love conquers all.

George Harris: Rebel with a cause: Eliza's husband. He heads up North—and makes it to freedom.

Harry ("Jim Crow"): Eliza's beautiful five-year-old son.

Arthur Shelby: The "good" plantation owner.

WHO'S
H
O
☞

> *(Continued)*
>
> **Topsy:** The ornery and cute little slave child whose main function is to underscore Eva's goodness.
>
> **Haley:** The villainous Southern slave trader who has the honor of chasing Eliza across the ice floes.
>
> **Cassy:** A slave on Legree's farm who terrorizes him with her "voodoo."

Tom has saved saccharine Eva from drowning and she has convinced her father to buy Tom.

Tom becomes head coachman for the St. Clares but spends most of his time with Little Eva, whose charm spreads faster than mono during freshman finals. She has touched the heart of Topsy, a scamp of a slave Eva's age. Eva grows more and more frail. Sensing that she is

UNCLE TOM'S CABIN MAKES THE BIG SCREEN

Avery Brooks, "Deep Space Nine's" Commander Sisko, and Phylicia Rashad of "The Cosby Show" fame headline in the 1987 movie of *Uncle Tom's Cabin*. It's missing the memorable Eliza-crossing-the-ice segment, but it does have a super cast, including a standout Edward Woodward as Simon Legree.

going to die, she begs her father to free the slaves, as he had long promised. Eva dies, and St. Clare is desolate. He makes plans to honor his daughter's deathbed wish but is killed in a brawl before he signs the papers. Mrs. St. Clare recovers from her imaginary illnesses long enough to put another coat of polish on her nails and to sell most of the slaves. Uncle Tom is put up for auction and sold to the most infamous villain in American literature: Simon Legree.

Tom tries to please his vicious master, but Legree nonetheless flogs him until he passes out. A slave named Cassy takes pity on Tom and comes to his aid. Cassy sneaks into Legree's attic and "haunts" him, but the beatings continue. Cassy and Emmeline, another slave, try to escape by tricking Legree, who mortally beats Tom trying to get the truth about the runaways. Two days later George Shelby arrives to buy Tom back, but he is too late. George buries Tom. On a riverboat headed toward Kentucky, Shelby meets Cassy and Emmeline, who have fled Legree. The women meet Madame de Thoux, George Harris's sister, and realize that Cassy is Eliza's mother.

The former slaves are reunited with their family in Canada. George Harris and his family travel to Liberia, Topsy returns to Vermont with St. Clare's sister. Shelby frees his slaves.

Uncle Tom's Cabin suffers from stereotyped characters and a plot that sometimes succeeds in spite of itself. Nonetheless, it was more influential and popular than the Big Mac—10,000 copies flew off the shelves the first week alone; 300,000, the first year. More than 1,500,000 copies sold in England; historians claim the book likely

ALL ABOARD FOR FREEDOM:
THE UNDERGROUND RAILROAD

The Underground Railroad was a loose network of anti-slavery Northerners who illegally helped slaves reach safety in the free states or in Canada. Begun by the Quakers in the 1780s, the network became well known in the 1830s. Among its most famous "conductors" were Harriet Tubman, a former slave called "Moses," and Levi Coffin, a Cincinnati Quaker. No one knows how many slaves reached freedom this way; estimates run as high as sixty thousand. Ultimately more important than the number arriving safely was the publicity generated, which helped make Northern whites aware of the evils of slavery and fuel the sectional mistrust that eventually led to the Civil War.

The Underground Railroad, a network of abolitionists who illegally spirited slaves to freedom

kept England from helping the South during the Civil War.

Uncle Tom's Cabin isn't great lit on the order of *Moby Dick* or *The Scarlet Letter*, but it wasn't intended to be. It is no news to anyone that *Uncle Tom's Cabin* is a polemic, a bible for the abolitionists. (You knew that.) With as much subtlety as electroshock therapy, the novel personalizes the evils of slavery. The suffering of Uncle Tom and Eliza tugged at the heartstrings of readers who had been unmoved by abolitionist rhetoric. Much of the novel, in fact, is based on thinly dis-

Uncle Tom's Cabin, *Harriet Beecher Stowe's masterpiece polemic*

guised true incidents; for the pathos, Stowe drew on her own misery.

Tom dies, as Mrs. Stowe believed Christ died, sustained by God and moved to bear his pain that others might live. Message Alert: The slavery crisis can only be resolved by Christian love. The reason that Tom is now regarded as a symbol of the cowardly, bootlicking slave is that he forgives Legree: "Mas'r, if you was sick, or in trouble, or dying, and I could save ye, I'd *give* ye my heart's blood; and, if taking every drop of blood in this poor old body would save your precious soul, I'd give 'em freely, as the Lord gave his for me." While today the book seems racist in its patronizing attitudes toward blacks, in 1852 *Uncle Tom's Cabin* was radical in its portrayal of the slaves' courage and dignity.

"A TOM SHOW"

Uncle Tom's Cabin reached an even wider audience in the form of a tearjerker of a melodrama that dozens of touring groups performed all over the country during the 1860s and 1870s. At one time in New York City alone, *Uncle Tom's Cabin* played eighteen times a week to sold-out houses. The play, often called "A Tom Show," was at best a first cousin to the novel, for characters and scenes were freely added. Ironically, the African-American characters were played by whites in blackface, for the presence of black actors (assuming some could have been found) performing on a stage viewed by whites would have been too shocking for the time. Stowe never saw the play or realized a cent from it.

OLDTOWN FOLKS:
WHAT'S LOVE GOT TO DO WITH IT?

Oldtown, Massachusetts is a developer's paradise, apt to make even the most jaded realtor toss aside his white wine spritzer and bolt for the cellular phone. It's all here, folks: the tranquil river that meanders through deep green hollows and hilltops, and the rustic Main Street, complete with clapboard meetinghouse, red-roofed schoolhouse, quaint general store, bustling tavern, and nifty general store. Add the warm neighbors and you'll think you've died and gone to heaven. Not quite—otherwise, there wouldn't be a story.

Horace Holyoke was ten when his father died. After the funeral Mrs. Holyoke took Horace and his brother, Bill, to live with her parents, Deacon and Mrs. Badger. The Badgers' home has overtones of Beirut, for the deacon and his good wife rarely see eye to eye on doctrinal matters. Horace and his brother learn to dodge flying missals, and get chummy with their aunts, Keziah and Lois, the former being the standard village spinster who is as homely as a post; the latter, tart and good-hearted.

Horace becomes friends with Harry Percival, the son of a feckless English officer who had deserted his wife and children, taking the marriage certificate and leaving behind a letter denying the legality of the marriage. Fundless and friendless, Mrs. Percival had tried to walk with Harry and daughter Eglantine (Tina) to Boston, an effort as romantic and ill-considered as the Crusades. On the way, she took sick and died in the house of Caleb Smith. Wrong move: Caleb decided to keep Harry as a field hand and send Tina to his sister,

**WHO'S
H
O** ☞

Oldtown Folks:
A LITERARY TOUT SHEET

Horace Holyoke: The narrator, a mensch who sticks around long enough to get the gal.

Deacon Badger: Horace's grandfather, a serene, affable cleric and farmer.

Mrs. Badger: The missus, a strict Calvinist as fond of theological dispute as she is of cleanliness.

Mr. Lothrop: The village minister.

Mrs. Lothrop: His wife.

Harry Percival: Horace's friend, who becomes (surprise) a minister.

Esther Avery: Harry's main squeeze, daughter of still another minister.

Eglantine (Tina) Percival: Harry's sister, a lovely young woman who turns out to be as good as she is beautiful.

Miss Mehitable Rossiter: Daughter of the former minister who adopts Tina and raises her as a daughter.

Emily Rossiter: Mehitable's younger half-sister, whose mysterious absence turns out to be a result of Major Sin.

**WHO'S
H
O**
☞

(*Continued*)

Ellery Davenport: The kind of guy to run off
with a twenty-two-year-old Lufthansa stewardess.

Miss Asphyxia, whose name says it all. Having wan-
dered into this grim fairy tale, the children promptly
wise up and hit the road. Deacon Badger and his wife
shelter the tykes and end up raising Harry. Soon after,
the kindly Miss Rossiter adopts Tina, in part to take
the place of sister Emily, who had mysteriously vanished several years before.

The children meet Ellery Davenport, Mrs. Lothrop's
handsome and clever cousin, who takes more than a
casual interest in the blossoming Tina. As the years
pass, suitors start to cluster around Tina like lawyers
at a hit-and-run. Tina and Harry are quickly dispatched
to boarding school, but it's neither fast nor far
enough—Tina and Ellery become engaged. The hon-
eymoon proves a bust: Emily Rossiter greets them at
their home and produces the child she had had years
ago with Ellery, which explains her vanishing act. Tina
nobly refuses to desert Ellery, instead using her fortune to support Emily. She takes the child with her
to England.

Meanwhile, Harry marries Esther Avery and moves to
England, where he inherits his father's land and title.
Eight years later Tina and Ellery return to Boston, Tina
looking like the "before" ad for Oil of Olay. Ellery continues his wanton ways and dies a decade later in a duel.

Two year later Horace and Tina marry and live happily ever after. Naturally, they visit Oldtown often.

A MOON-DUST-IN-YOUR-HAIR KIND OF PLACE

Since it's plain that plot went down for the count on this one, what did *Oldtown Folks* do to deserve the big ink? Stowe's first biographer (also her son) believed that *Oldtown Folks* was destined to endure, and subsequent critics not related by blood have confirmed his judgment. Like Cinderella, *Oldtown Folks* had a hard time making it to the prom, but once it got there, it stole Prince Charming's heart. For decades *Uncle Tom's Cabin* overshadowed the gentle *Oldtown Folks*; only now are readers beginning to appreciate the book for its vivid picture of the changing social life of New England life shortly after the Revolutionary War and its realistic treatment of time, place, and character. The novel paved the way for such later works as the local-color novels of Sarah Orne Jewett and Edgar Lee Masters's *Spoon River Anthology*.

In *Oldtown Folks*, Stowe succeeds in bringing to life the ambience of a small New England town. She takes great pains to describe the three religious persuasions—Calvinism, Arminianism, and Episcopalianism—that manage to coexist, if not always peacefully. Today we're uneasy when religion dominates life, but Stowe's balancing act reminds us that this was once the norm, not the exception. Despite its slightly ancient air, *Oldtown Folks* reminds us of the virtue of tolerance.

To modern critics, the novel's only flaw is its sentimentality: Stowe's irresistible urge to marry Horace and Tina at the end of the story. This happily-ever-after ending smacks of artificiality in an otherwise gritty portrayal of real life.

EDGAR LEE MASTERS (1868–1950)

In 1915 practicing lawyer Edgar Lee Masters burst on to the literary scene like a sonic bomb: *Spoon River Anthology* had nineteen printings in its first edition alone, unprecedented for poetry. Originally conceived as a novel, the *Anthology* is a series of poetic monologues by 244 former inhabitants (both real and imagined) of Spoon River, an area near Petersburg, Illinois, where Masters spent much of his childhood. The whole cast is dead, and from the grave they speak their own epitaphs. In addition to rigor mortis, death brings with it freedom from censure, so Masters's fictional speakers can freely express their hatreds, despair, and resentment at life's slings and arrows. The poems' unsentimental depiction of private lives, acceptance of sex, and critical view of America and small town life outraged the public and helped spark the Chicago Renaissance, a movement to establish Hog Town as the literary place to be.

SUMMARY

Created one of the most powerful documents in American letters (don't make us call it a novel), whose characters have become part of the American imagination.

Fashioned realistic literature with a regional flavor.

Churned out delicious four-hanky tearjerkers.

Frederick Douglass, 1817–1895,
American lecturer, writer, and abolitionist

CHAPTER 7

FREDERICK DOUGLASS

(1817–1895)

YOU MUST REMEMBER THIS

Douglass, an escaped slave, became one of the most effective orators of his day, an influential newspaper writer, a militant abolitionist, and a famous diplomat. The Abbie Hoffman of the slave set.

MOST FAMOUS FOR

Being a one-book kind of guy who did all his own research. He wrote one book and expanded it twice, each time bringing the reader up to date with his life. Here it is, in all three versions:

★ *Narrative of the Life of Frederick Douglass, an American Slave. Written by Himself* (1845)

★ *My Bondage and My Freedom* (1855) [enlarged version of previous book]

★ *The Life and Times of Frederick Douglass* (1881) [see above]

REBEL WITH A CAUSE

66 **I** appear this evening as a thief and a robber,"
announced Frederick Douglass at an antislavery meeting in 1842. "I stole this head, these
limbs, this body from my master, and ran off with them."
With such pathos and outrage, Douglass evoked the suffering of slavery. This guy really knew how to work a
room. A shame that his material was such a downer.

He was born Frederick Augustus Washington Bailey
on one of the wealthiest plantations in Maryland, but he
remained unimpressed with the wealthy spread. Later in
life he would describe his birthplace as "a small district
of country, thinly populated, and remarkable for nothing
I know of more than the worn-out sandy, desert-like ap-
pearance of its soil." His mother, Harriet Bailey, was
literate, and according to the grapevine, his father was
the master himself, Captain Anthony. Young Frederick
was raised in relative happiness by his grandmother in
her cabin. When he was six, however, he was dispatched
to the main plantation, where he and the other small
slave children were put into a breeding pen with dogs
and pigs. They were called "pigs" and fed cornmeal
mush, which they scooped from a trough with spoons
improvised from oyster shells or pieces of old shingles.

When he was about nine, young Bailey was sent to
Baltimore to care for Hugh and Lucretia Auld's young
son, Tommy. At first Bailey got along well with Mrs.
Auld, because she did not know the "proper" way to
manage a slave. As a result, she treated Bailey like her
own child, even teaching him to read. Mr. Auld quickly
set his missus on the right path—"If he learns to read,
it will forever unfit him to be a slave," Auld rightly de-

creed—and she was forced to discontinue the reading lessons. But Bailey thirsted for knowledge. He tricked neighborhood white boys into giving him lessons and read Tommy's schoolbooks on the sly. Through the daily newspaper he learned of the abolition movement, which fired his desire to be free.

ABOLITIONISM

Most historians cite 1831 as the beginning of the abolitionist movement in America, when William Lloyd Garrison founded *The Liberator*, soon to become the leading antislavery newspaper. The movement gained power with the passage of the Fugitive Slave Act in 1850 and, seven years later, the Dred Scott Case, which ruled that blacks were not U.S. citizens. Well-known abolitionists included Stephen S. Foster, Abby Kelley, Charles Lenox Redmond, Wendell Phillips, Angelina and Sarah Grimké, James Russell Lowell, and Frances E. W. Harper, who expressed their opposition to slavery in poetry, prose, and lectures.

In 1833, when he was fifteen, Bailey was shipped to another plantation. When he refused to step-and-fetchit with sufficient speed, the teen was sent to the notorious "slave breaker" Edward Covey. While suffering one especially vicious beating, Bailey decided to fight back. Two hours later Covey gave up, but not without snarling, "Now, you scoundrel, go to your work. I would not have whipped you so hard if you had not resisted." Bailey decided that it was time to seek his freedom.

On September 3, 1838, Bailey escaped from slavery. Disguised as a free sailor, he made it to New York and from there took a trip on the Underground Railroad to

Massachusetts. He was joined by a woman from Baltimore who had helped him flee, Anna Murray, and they married. To make recapture harder, Frederick Bailey changed his name to Frederick Douglass, after a character in a novel by Sir Walter Scott.

SIR WALTER SCOTT (1771–1832)

We have Scott to thank for paving the way for such socially significant genres as airport fiction and bodice rippers; we'd like to pin soap operas on him as well, but it's a stretch. His career got a jump start with long narrative poems like "The Lady of the Lake" (1810), the source of Our Hero's new handle. Less than ten years later, Scott gave up poetry for novels because, he said, "Byron beat me." *Waverly* kicked off the dance, and the historical novel was born. When the smoke cleared, Scott had become the most famous and most prolific English writer of his day. Peruse *Rob Roy* (1817) or *The Bride of Lammermoor* (1819) for an idea of what a juicy novel *ought* to be. Eat your heart out, Barbara Cartland.

A few months later, Douglass was roped into speaking at an antislavery convention, and a media darling was born. The personal risk was staggering—nothing like publicity to make recapture more likely—and even in the North abolitionists were about as popular as body lice.

Introduced as "a piece of property" or a "graduate of that peculiar institution, with his diploma written on his back," Douglass traveled throughout the North delivering passionate accounts of his years in bondage. His flashing eyes, large mass of hair, and well-defined pecs added to the drama. In 1845 he set down the story of his life, and a bestseller was born. But every party has a pooper, and here we had the proslavery folk, who agitated for Douglass's recapture. No fool he, Douglass traveled to England to spread the word until the heat died down. In 1846 his supporters purchased his freedom for $750. Soon after, he sailed home, a free man at last.

FEMINISM

Douglass attended the first women's rights convention in 1848 and was a lifelong supporter of the women's movement. The abolitionists, suffragettes, and temperance leaders were a tight bunch. Even Rush Limbaugh wouldn't mud-wrestle the female political activists of the day—Susan B. Anthony, Lucretia Mott, Elizabeth Cady Stanton—women as handy with an ax as they were with a ballot.

The First Feminists: Elizabeth Cady Stanton and Susan B Anthony

In 1847 Douglass created *The North Star*, an abolitionist newspaper. Like all worthy causes, it hemorrhaged money, and despite a name change, the paper limped along for more than a decade before gasping its last. Throughout, Douglass continued his work with abolitionists John Brown, Sojourner Truth, and others.

Douglass worked tirelessly to ensure that the Civil War would not only preserve the Union but also free all slaves. He assisted in the recruitment of the first black regiment, the Massachusetts 54th, and his sons Lewis and Charles were among the first to enlist. For his efforts, Douglass became the most famous and well-respected black leader in the country. He not only made the A-list for White House parties but was also able to buy the manor to which he wasn't born. In 1876 President Hayes appointed him a United States

SOJOURNER TRUTH (1797–1883)

Sojourner Truth, 1797-1883, American abolitionist: The Moses of her People

An illiterate slave who ran away from her New York master in the 1820s, Isabella Baumfree began calling herself "Sojourner Truth" because, she said, God intended her to "travel up and down the land, showing the people their sins, and being a sign unto them." Tall, gaunt, and dynamic, she became a popular speaker at abolitionist rallies. Her plain speaking about the evils of slavery moved many audiences, and her wit silenced those who dared challenge her. After one speech a listener demanded, "Old woman, do you think that your talk about slavery does any good? Why, I don't care any more for your talk than I do for the bite of a flea."

"Perhaps not," replied Sojourner Truth, "but, de Lord willin', I'll keep you scratchin'."

marshal; in 1889 President Harrison appointed him U.S. minister to Haiti. He served in both positions with great distinction and dignity. He died of a heart attack in 1895, agitating to the last.

Excerpt from *Narrative of the Life of Frederick Douglass, an American Slave*

I was born in Tuckahoe, near Hillsborough, and about twelve miles from Easton, in Talbot county, Maryland. I have no accurate knowledge of my age, never having seen any authentic record containing it. By far the larger part of the slaves know as little of their ages as horses know of theirs, and it is the wish of most masters within my knowledge to keep their slaves thus ignorant. . . .

As to my own treatment while I lived on Colonel Lloyd's plantation, it was very similar to that of the other slave children. I was not old enough to work in the field, and there being little else than field work to do, I had a great deal of leisure time. The most I had to do was drive up the cows at evening, keep the fowls out of the garden, keep the front yard clean, and run errands for my old master's daughter, Mrs. Lucretia Auld. The most of my leisure time I spent in helping Master Daniel Lloyd in finding his birds, after he had shot them. My connection to Master Daniel was of some advantage to me. He became quite attached to me, and was sort of a protector to me. He would not allow the older boys to impose on me, and would divide his cakes with me.

I was seldom whipped by my old master, and suffered little from any thing else than hunger and cold. I suffered much from hunger, but much more from cold. In hottest summer and coldest winter, I was kept almost naked—no shoes, no stockings, no jacket, no trousers, nothing but a coarse tow linen shirt, reaching only to my knees. I had no bed. I must have perished head and feet out. My feet have been so cracked with the frost, that the pen with which I am writing might be laid in gashes. . . .

Tsunami of a Tale

In 125 pages of deceptively simple narrative, Douglass re-creates the story of his life from early childhood until his escape from slavery when he was twenty-one years old. The book was a hit on both continents, and was translated into both French and German. "It is an excellent piece of writing," the *New York Tribune* declared, "and on that score to be prized as a specimen of powers of the black race, which prejudice persists in disputing."

Inevitably, a handful of people with the collective IQ of a sardine claimed that a slave could not have written such a powerful book. Several ghostwriters floating around were given credit, but anyone who had heard Douglass speak—and by then they numbered in the thousands—recognized the passion and language of the book as genuine. The great white father of the antislavery movement, William Lloyd Garrison, contributed a Preface to the text. His contribution served to authenticate the book. "Mr. Douglass," Garrison wrote, "has very properly chosen to write his own Narrative, in his own style, and according to the best of his ability, rather than employ someone else." With a public relations eye that would shame pitchmasters on the Home Shopping Channel, Garrison's Preface also served to make Douglass's life still further ammunition in the antislavery war.

WILLIAM LLOYD GARRISON (1805–1879)

The most radical of the militant abolitionists, Garrison gained the honor of having a price on his head for his antislavery stance: in 1831 the state of Georgia anted up $5,000 for Garrison's arrest and conviction. Undaunted, he denounced the Constitution as "a covenant with Death and an agreement with Hell" and burned it publicly. He made his point.

William Lloyd Garrison, 1807-1879, the most radical of the militant abolitionists

The power of Douglass's *Narrative* rests in large part on its moral force—a triumph of courage and dignity over the brutality of slavery. More than an autobiography, it is a sermon on how slavery corrupts the human spirit and robs both master and slave of their freedom.

Douglass's autobiography is in the tradition of the slave narrative, a genre that dates from the early 1600s. Olaudah Equiano's *Interesting Narrative of the Life of Olaudah Equiano, or Gustavus Vassa, the African* (1789) and Booker T. Washington's *Up from Slavery: An Autobiography* (1901) are shelved alongside Douglass's *Narrative*, but

AFRICAN-AMERICAN LITERATURE

Frederick Douglass hit a home run with his autobiography, but there are some other heavy hitters on the black lit syllabus. Jupiter Hammond (1711–1790?) was the literary Jackie Robinson, the first black writer to smash the color line and make it into print. Phillis Wheatley (1753?–1784) gets the nod as the first female black

Phillis Wheatley, 1753?-1784, America's first female African-American writer

writer in America. Charles W. Chesnutt (1858–1932), W. E. B. Du Bois (1868–1963), and Paul Laurence Dunbar (1872–1906), Ralph Ellison (1914–1994), James Baldwin (1924–1987), Zora Neale Hurston (1891–1960), and Langston Hughes (1903–1967) all wrote powerful works. The dean of modern black writers, Richard Wright (1908–1960), suspected J. Edgar was tailing him as a Commie and he was; Toni Morrison (1931–   ), Alice Walker (1944–   ), and Gwendolyn Brooks (1917–   ) are no less talented for not making it to the government's Most Wanted List. In 1993 Morrison received the Nobel Prize for Literature, the first black American so honored.

Our Hero's book has the distinction of being ranked as the finest example of the slave autobiography as a literary art form. The kid outran being a runaway, for his autobiography is now read less as a story of slavery than as a story of self. Like Whitman's song of himself or Melville's story of surviving in a world at sea with evil, the *Narrative* is a story of self-emancipation.

My Bondage and My Freedom

My Bondage and My Freedom takes up where the *Narrative* left off. In this installment of truth and consequences, Douglass traces his work with Garrison and his followers, his sold-out speaking tours through the United Kingdom, the purchase of his freedom, and his move to Rochester, New York. He describes how in December of 1847 he started his newspaper, first called *The North Star*, later, *Frederick Douglass' Paper*. This version of his autobiography includes more of his feelings and philosophies than the *Narrative*, but like the volume to follow, the story is essentially the same.

What's different is Douglass's self-confidence: *My Bondage and My Freedom* can be seen as its author's declaration of independence. While Douglass denied none of the praise for William Lloyd Garrison that appears in the *Narrative*, neither did he solicit a letter of introduction to open this volume. The text is far more critical than its predecessor.

The Life and Times of Frederick Douglass

The Life and Times of Frederick Douglass shows editing used to advantage. A combination of books one and two, this volume updates the *Life* with news from the front and describes a justly famous man enjoying his honors while still smarting from the wrongs he suffered.

Douglass was reminding people that the story of slavery could not be so easily forgotten—it must remain indelibly etched in the national conscience. Douglass saw his life as a symbol of the former slaves who were not yet fully free, no matter what was written on a piece of paper. Social, economic, and political problems remained unsolved.

But it didn't really matter. He had said his piece, and America had listened when it counted. See, sometimes the good guys *do* win in the end.

SUMMARY

- Was the most famous, revered African American of the nineteenth century.

- Was the most effective abolitionist of his day.

- Founded and ran an influential newspaper.

- Became a renowned diplomat.

Walt Whitman, 1819-1892,
freed verse—and himself—from the constraints of society

CHAPTER 8

WALT WHITMAN
(1819–1892)

YOU MUST REMEMBER THIS

Whitman did for poetry what Howard Stern does for radio: stand it on its ear. Stern's hair is cleaner, but Whitman's book is better.

MOST FAMOUS FOR

Creating new poetic forms, now poetic subjects, and lending his name to assorted malls, high schools, and banks across Long Island. He wrote only one really famous book—*Leaves of Grass*—but churned out nine different versions. The final edition contains 389 poems. The other two books—*Democratic Vistas* (1871) and *Specimen Days* (1882)—are also worth a look.

A BARBARIC YAWP

Whitman was about as subtle as Madonna, but not nearly as firm. Like the Material Girl, he was a tireless self-promoter who raised chutzpah to an art form. For example, he thought nothing of writing his own reviews (under an assumed name, natch) and coauthoring his own biography, *The Good Gray Poet* (1866). With a skill every junior senator might envy, Whitman managed to become the most photographed poet of his century, perhaps of all time.

He was equally blatant about his views, declaring in "Song of Myself":

> I celebrate myself, and sing myself,
> And what I assume you shall assume,
> For every atom belonging to me
>   as good as belongs to you.

That self was a part of all humanity and especially of the United States. Clearly on the inside curve of a major twentieth-century trend, he believed that sexuality was the most vital aspect of life and should be expressed openly. The "hankering, gross, mystical nude," as he called himself, trumpeted his "barbaric yawp" around the world and took off his clothes a lot. The man had carnal knowledge of everything but a McCormick reaper.

The Long Island native left school at eleven and held a number of McJobs—office boy, gofer, printer's assistant—before beginning to write. He completed his education at newspaper offices on Long Island, rising through the ranks of the *Brooklyn Eagle* to become editor in 1846. Two years later, he upped sticks, heading south to New Orleans for a spell. Returning to Sodom-on-the

Hudson, he did a turn as a house builder and infuriated his parents by reading instead of taking out the trash.

Whitman burst onto the literary scene in 1855 with the publication of *Leaves of Grass*. In the opening manifesto, he declared that the new American poet (guess who) would create new forms and subject matter for poetry, rejecting conventional language, rhythm, and rhyme. In order to approximate the rhythms of oratorical speech, he would write in long lines. He would weave together vocabularies from many walks of life, speaking in a voice larger than life, a bardic voice he meant to represent both himself and all of America. Henceforth, American poetry would deal with reality, not highfalutin moral lessons.

But the essay didn't quite prepare readers for the psychologically complex, intense, and sexually explicit poems that followed. Not surprisingly, the book didn't exactly fly off the shelves. To poke a little spark into the embers, Whitman sent a copy of *Leaves of Grass* to the head poetry honcho, Ralph Waldo Emerson. The resident sage gave the upstart a jump start. "I am not blind," Emerson wrote, "to the worth of the wonderful gift of *Leaves of Grass*. I find it the most extraordinary piece of wit and wisdom that America has yet contributed." Whitman promptly slapped the endorsement on the back cover of the second edition, but somehow never got around to requesting Emerson's permission. Unfazed by his own impudence, the poet next wrote an open letter to Emerson of his determination "to meet people and The States face to face, to confront them with an American rude tongue." Along the way, he inflated sales figures, planned future print runs, and generally ran off at the mouth. None of this got him nominated for Prom

King. The literary establishment turned an icy shoulder: Henry Wadsworth Longfellow, Oliver Wendell Holmes, Sr., James Russell Lowell, Henry David Thoreau, and Bronson Alcott refused to consider him part of their circle.

HOOKED ON SONNETS

Longfellow and his fellow "Fireside Poets" (Holmes, Lowell, and John Greenleaf Whittier) penned soothing little ditties that families could intone over the hearth. One of their favorite forms was the sonnet, a lyric poem of fourteen lines written in iambic pentameter, a rhythm with five accents in each line. Originated by Italian poets during the thirteenth century, the form reached perfection a century later in the works of Petrarch and came to be known as the "Petrarchan," or "Italian," sonnet. The first eight lines, called the "octave," rhyme a-b-b-a, a-b-b-a and present the problem; the concluding six lines, called the "sestet," rhyme c-d-e, c-d-e and resolve the problem. Sixteenth-century English poets swiped the idea but changed the rhyme to a-b-a-b, c-d-c-d, e-f-e-f, g-g. Shakespeare pounced on the form and succeeded in doing for the love sonnet what Godiva did for chocolate.

Whitman, unfazed by the snub, hung out instead with a motley crew of drivers and theater people and planned the third edition of *Leaves of Grass*. He served as a nurse during the Civil War, where his heroic efforts as a wound-dresser earned him widespread respect and gratitude. His book was published in England, and our man in gray became something of a literary lion. In 1873 a serious stroke doomed Whitman to a cruel existence: he was forced to live in New Jersey. The invalid made the best of life in Camden, helped along by fan mail from Alfred Lord Tennyson, England's poet laureate.

Whitman died in 1892, recognized throughout America as the poet who had given his country its first lyrical voice, one that was uniquely American. He is buried in Camden, New Jersey.

"CROSSING BROOKLYN FERRY"

1
Flood-tide below me! I see you face to face!
Clouds of the west—sun there half an hour high—
I see you also face to face.

Crowds of men and women attired in the usual
costumes, how curious you are to me!
On the ferry-boats the hundreds and hundreds
that cross, returning home, are more curious
to me than you suppose,
And you that shall cross from shore to shore
years hence are more to me, and more
in my meditations, than you might suppose.

ALL ABOARD!

"Crossing Brooklyn Ferry," which first appeared in 1856 under the title "Sun-Down Poem," describes a literal ferry crossing between Brooklyn and Manhattan aboard the *Fulton Street Ferry*. The narrator imagines the vast cityscape as it might appear to a person centuries in the future. Meanwhile, below deck, you've got the metaphorical meaning: strip away the "usual costumes" and you see what binds all people together in the Big Picture. Like the feeling of grooving at a really happening concert, Whitman experiences the feeling of merging the soul with a larger reality. He offers the comforting vision of a "well-joined scheme" in which every part of reality contributes to the unification of the spirit of humanity, like the satisfied feeling you get after eating an entire pint of chocolate almond chip ice cream.

Brooklyn Ferry, mid 19th century

FREE VERSE

Free verse is not poetry marked way down for a quick sale—it's poetry written without a regular pattern of rhyme and meter. This kind of verse uses a rhythm that reinforces the meaning and the sounds of spoken language in lines of different length. Whitman gets the nod

FREE VERSE *(continued)*

as the inventor of the form. Noted word slinger Robert
Frost, a good ol' boy from Vermont, said writing free
verse is like playing tennis with the net down.

*"Two roads diverged in a wood . . . and I took
the one less traveled."*

"I SING THE BODY ELECTRIC"

1

I sing the body electric,
The armies of those I love engirth me and I en-
girth them,
They will not let me off till I go with them, respond
to them,
And discorrupt them, and charge them full with the
charge of the soul. . . .
5
This is the female form,
A divine nimbus exhales from it head to foot,

It attracts with fierce undeniable attraction,

I am drawn by its breadth as if I were no more than
a helpless vapor, all falls aside but myself and it,

Books, art, religion, time, the visible and solid earth,
and what was expected of heaven or fear'd of hell,
are now consumed,

Mad filaments, ungovernable shoots play out of it,
the response likewise ungovernable,

Hair, bosom, hips, bend of legs, negligent falling
hands all diffused, mine too diffused,

Ebb stung by the flow and flow stung by the ebb,
love-flesh swelling and deliciously aching,

Limitless limpid jets of love hot and enormous, quivering jelly of love, white-blow and delirious juice,

Bridegroom night of love, working surely and softly
into the prostrate dawn . . .

NAUGHTY BITS

"I Sing the Body Electric" first appeared in the 1860
edition of *Leaves of Grass*, as the third poem of the "Children of Adam" sequence. This hymn in praise of human
sexuality caused an uproar. The Sultan of Sweat's homoerotic longings were not a real résumé-builder.

The first four lines describe the connectedness of everything the poet loves. In section 2 he describes the
entire body, top to bottom, concluding with a statement
of his unity with it all. Section 3 describes a vigorous
farmer; section 4, the body's feel and smell. Section 5
extols the virtues of the female body; section 6 gives
equal time to the male body. At the end of these sec-

tions, Whitman argues forcefully for the equality of all people. Sections 7 and 8 are set in a slave auction, which reads better than it plays to twentieth-century sensibilities. The final section is a long catalog of the parts of the human body, a poetic owner's manual for the human body. The body and soul are united with each other and the poem: bodies are "the soul," and "they are my poems," Whitman declares.

THE CATALOG

The catalog technique in poetry predates Sears and Montgomery Ward—Homer used it around 800 B.C., John Milton in the seventeenth century; greedy children use it around Christmas. It's nothing more than a list, but when used with brio, it's as overwhelming as Toys "R" Us on Christmas Eve. Whitman had it down pat.

FLASH AND CLASH

"I Sing the Body Electric" was too racy for most nineteenth-century readers; even Emerson, Whitman's staunch supporter, advised him to cut it out of the book. But Whitman refused to bend his principles for anyone. Sexuality, he believed, should not be concealed, for it was one of the most vital aspects of life. As a result, he not only included "I Sing the Body Electric" but also added the homoerotic "Calamus" poems. Predictably, Whitman's fidelity to his craft affected all aspects of his life. Many years later Whitman was fired from a government post after his superiors stumbled upon these X-rated gems.

"A NOISELESS PATIENT SPIDER"

A noiseless patient spider,
I mark'd where on the little promontory
   it stood isolated,
Mark'd how to explore the vacant vast surrounding,
It launch'd forth filament, filament, filament,
   out of itself,
Ever unreeling them, ever tirelessly speeding them.

And you O my soul where you stand,
Surrounded, detached, in measureless
   oceans of space,
Ceaselessly musing, venturing, throwing,
   seeking the spheres to connect them,
Till the bridge you will need be form'd,
   till the ductile anchor hold,
Till the gossamer thread you fling
   catch somewhere, O my soul.

BLACK WIDOW BLUES

The poem begins with a minor incident: a spider, alone on a cliff, throws out its filaments into space. But here's the difference between us and Whitman: we'd use last week's *Sports Illustrated* to squash the sucker flatter than a Ritz, but Whitman knew this was a Poetic Moment with Cosmic Meaning. Sure enough, in the second stanza, the spider's activity becomes a metaphor symbolizing the poet's search for immortality. The poet sends out his verse as the spider his web, both hoping to connect and so give their lives meaning. It is rarely that easy to find meaning in life, as the inconclusive ending shows.

  This is a lonely-guy poem, as pitiful as a half-nuked

Lean Cuisine and a warm six-pack on a Saturday night. The spider becomes a symbol of the pathetic plight of humanity, desperately seeking meaning. What makes this a great poem? It's the attempt itself, which captures the heroic dignity of the human soul, hanging from a slender thread over the abyss of chaos.

"WHEN LILACS LAST IN THE DOORYARD BLOOM'D"

1

When lilacs last in the dooryard bloom'd,
And the great star early dropp'd
  in the western sky in the night,
I mourn'd, and yet shall mourn
  with ever-returning spring.
Ever-returning spring, trinity sure to me you bring,
Lilac blooming perennial and drooping star
  in the west,
And thought of him I love.

ASIDE FROM THAT, MRS. LINCOLN, HOW DID YOU LIKE THE PLAY?

Whitman wrote this elegy a few weeks after Lincoln's assassination on April 14, 1865. The sixteen numbered sections of free verse express his grief over Lincoln's death and his attempt to transform the tragedy into an understanding of the cycle of life and death. Sections 1 and 2 lament the President's death, while section 3 shifts the focus to a lilac bush in the dooryard. Section 4 brings in the image of a warbling thrush; section 5, Lincoln's

The Assassination of Abraham Lincoln, April 14, 1865

coffin and society's grief. In sections 7–14, Whitman merges his sorrow with society's. Sections 14–15 bring in images of death from the Civil War and transform suffering into visions of peace and rest. The conclusion shows that Whitman has found a way to deal with his grief through nature:

> Lilac and star and bird twined
>   with the chant of my soul,
> There in the fragrant pines
>   and the cedars dusk and dim.

Whitman saw Lincoln as the representative democratic man, the living symbol of his own message to America. The poem succeeds in transforming his personal grief into an expression of national mourning. Implicit in this process is Whitman's belief that the real meaning of Lincoln's death is so vast that it can be grasped only by poetry, not through rational thought. The lilacs symbolize the everlasting spring (the poet's love), the fallen western star represents Lincoln, and the song of the hermit thrush stands for the universalization of the poet's grief.

"PASSAGE TO INDIA"

7

Passage indeed O soul to primal thought,
Not lands and seas alone, thy own clear freshness,
The young maturity of brood and bloom,
To realms of budding bibles.

O soul, repressless, I wish thee and thou with me,
Thy circumnavigation of the world begin,
Of man, the voyage of his mind's return,
To reason's early paradise,
Back, back to wisdom's birth,
    to innocent intuitions,
Again with fair creation.

CRUISING WITH WALT

When Whitman finally finished obsessing over these verses, he ended up with a 255-line poem in nine sections. The work opens with a description of the three big Tinkertoys of the time: the laying of the transatlantic cable (1866), the completion of the first transcontinental railroad (1869), and the opening of the Suez Canal (1869). Science becomes metaphor: as these nifty creations connect the world materially, so Whitman's poem links the world spiritually. The poet takes a quantum leap through time to pay homage to history's vast panorama.

The passage to India, which that imperialistic slime Columbus sought and the narrator now resumes, is transformed into the voyage of "primal thought." The poet metaphorically circumnavigates the world in an effort to return to the Transcendental utopia of intuition and literary creation. The insistent tone and repetition combine to create an almost religious effect that has, like the world it describes, a "hidden prophetic intention."

NEITHER A BORROWER NOR A LENDER BE?

In 1924 Brit wussy E. M. Forster used *Passage to India* as the title of his fifth and last novel, an existential morass about finding meaning in a meaningless world. Master sci-fi maven Ray Bradbury swiped the title "I Sing the Body Electric" and slapped it on a story that has justly become a classic. Even that trendy rag *Vanity Fair* got into the act, describing a pumped-up Sylvester Stallone as "the body electric." Caution: When an undergraduate appropriates a section of a literary work it's called "plagiarism"; when a literary great does it, it's called "homage."

"OUT OF THE CRADLE ENDLESSLY ROCKING"

Out of the cradle endlessly rocking,
Out of the mocking-bird's throat, the musical shuttle,
Out of the Ninth-month midnight,
Over the sterile sands and the fields beyond, where the child leaving the bed wander'd alone, bareheaded, barefooted,

Down from the shower'd halo,
Up from the mystic play of shadows twining and
 twisting as if they were alive,
Out from the patches of briers and blackberries,
From the memories of the bird that chanted to
 me . . .
A man, yet by these tears a little boy again,
Throwing myself on the sand, confronting the
 waves,
I, chanter of pains and joys, uniter of here and
 hereafter,
Taking all hints to use them, but swiftly leaping
 beyond them,
A reminiscence sing.

ROCK AROUND THE CLOCK

"Out of the Cradle Endlessly Rocking" is a poem about
memory, a biggie with the Romantics. Like Wordsworth's
"Lines: Composed a Few Miles Above Tintern Abbey"
and Longfellow's "My Lost Youth," Whitman's "Out of
the Cradle Endlessly Rocking" explores how childhood
prepared the poet to assume the mantle of Art. The
poem opens with a description of Long Island, which he
calls by the Indian name "Paumanok," and his childhood there.

The end of the poem focuses on the poet's listening
to the ocean's song of death, but for Whitman, death is
not a one-way ticket to Palookaville. Instead, death is a
natural part of the cycle of life, as the poem's strong
rhythm and repetition suggests. Walt got it all together
in this poem: the form of the poem echoes its content.
Look again at the first three lines: each opens with the

LAWN GUYLAND

· ·

A slender 119-mile spit of land jutting into the cool green Atlantic, the birthplace of suburban sprawl nurtured literary heavyweights F. Scott Fitzgerald and Ring Lardner, educated trendy comedian Jerry Seinfeld, polished hunky Alec Baldwin, and raised warblers Billy Joel and Mariah Carey. All this was before the Guyland spawned *The Amityville Horror*, Joey Buttafuoco, and Joel Rifkin, as well as a motley assortment of lesser-known homicidal maniacs, adulterers, and perverts. Bring the whole family.

F. Scott Fitzgerald, 1896-1940, American novelist and short story writer who epitomized mood and manners of the 1920s "Jazz Age"

word "out," and the poem rocks with a rhythm Elvis would envy. The images also reinforce the cyclical nature of existence. The rocking cradle, the singing bird, the youthful poet, and the sea recur throughout, reminding readers of life's constancy and its change.

"SCENTED HERBAGE OF MY BREAST"

Scented herbage of my breast,
Leaves from you I glean, I write,
    to be perused best afterwards,

Tomb-leaves, body-leaves growing up
   above me above death,
Perennial roots, tall leaves, O the winter
   shall not freeze you delicate leaves,
Every year shall you bloom again, out from
   where you retired you shall emerge again;
O I do not know whether many passing by
   will discover you or inhale your faint odor,
   but I believe a few will;
O slender leaves! O blossoms of my blood!
   I permit you to tell in your own way
   of the heart that is under you . . .

GRASS

As the golden arches are to the Big Mac, so grass is to
the Big Poet. The speaker, a hearty man's man, literally,
first notes the timelessness of the grass, which endures
winter's icy blasts and summer's blazing heat. The grass
reminds him of death, love, and life, all interconnected
into a great cycle of existence. He then addresses death,
seeing it as "the real reality." The lyric moves from the
specific symbol of the grass to the abstraction of death,
from material to spiritual reality, from the particular to
the universal, and so grass becomes a symbol of the cyclic
quality of nature and humanity.

The poem is part of the "Calamus" section of *Leaves
of Grass*, calamus being a very large, sweet-smelling grass.
When the poem's speaker waxes lyrical over the grass,
he is really celebrating the aroma and heartiness of life.

SUMMARY

- Created free verse, poetry without a set rhythm or rhyme.

- Showed American writers and readers that it was not necessary to imitate European models.

- Encouraged those who came after to write about their own society in their own way.

- Gave America a myth.

- Lent his name to a lot of public buildings.

Herman Melville, 1819-1891,
creator of what is arguably America's greatest novel, Moby-Dick

CHAPTER 9

HERMAN MELVILLE

(1819–1891)

YOU MUST REMEMBER THIS

Moby Dick (1851) leads the pack as America's greatest novel; Melville, as our greatest novelist.

MOST FAMOUS FOR

A really big book about a really big fish, but his other books also make a good read:

★ *Typee* (1846)
★ *Omoo* (1847)
★ *Mardi* (1849)
★ *Redburn* (1849)
★ *White Jacket* (1850)
★ *Pierre* (1852)

★ *The Piazza Tales* (1856)
★ *The Confidence Man* (1857)
★ *Battle Pieces* (1866)
★ *Clarel* (1876)
★ *Billy Budd* (1924;
  published posthumously)

MAN OVERBOARD

Herman Melville made his debut August 1, 1819, the third child of Allan Melvill, a prosperous importer of elegant French goods. Both Allan and his wife, the former Maria Gansevoort, came from money and often made the New York scene. Long on personal charm but short on common sense, Allan plundered his inheritance to stave off bankruptcy, but by 1830 the business had run aground. Creditors stormed the gates two days past Herman's eleventh birthday. By then there were eight little Melvilles and lots of shoes to buy. Mentally and physically shattered, Allan died two years later. Left in financial limbo, the family moved to a small town near Troy, New York. Maria decided to spin-doctor the family name, adding an *e* at the end to improve their social rep in the society pages.

Herman's education was spotty at best. His mother, never one to hold back her opinions, noted that her darling "does not appear so fond of his Books as to injure his Health," and so took him out of school when he was twelve. Herman worked at a variety of menial jobs to help Maria maintain the style of living to which she had become accustomed. When he was eighteen, Herman tried teaching, but anxious to escape from his students and Mother Dearest, he quickly signed on the *St. Lawrence*, a British merchant ship. He managed to stretch his parole from Mama to five years but finally had to return home. He made a brief foray West, but the mail still got through. In 1841 he dumped his mother's demands into his brother's lap and set sail for the Pacific aboard a whaling ship.

A whaler's life was not all guns and roses, however, so

Melville and a shipmate jumped ship at the Marquesas Islands. After a brief sojourn with a tribe of cheerful natives who turned out to be cheerful cannibals, he escaped on an Australian whaler, hopping off at Tahiti. From there it was a simple hitch to Hawaii and home. In 1844 he began to write about his exotic adventures.

*Club Med, circa 1800s, the setting for
Melville's early blockbusters* Typee *and* Omoo

His tales of cannibal banquets and nubile native girls—*Typee* and *Omoo*—delighted readers and reviewers alike. The *Brooklyn Eagle*'s literary critic, one Walt Whitman, called *Omoo* "thorough entertainment." In 1847 Melville married Elizabeth Shaw and settled in New York City. Flush with success and love, he wrote *Mardi*, a demanding allegorical novel that repulsed his fans. "Bring on the hula girls," they clamored. Melville acquiesced, producing *Redburn* and *White Jacket*. The bank balance back in the black, he bought a 160-acre Massachusetts farm. Despairing that he was doomed to be remembered only as "the man who had lived among the cannibals," and encouraged by his friendship with neighbor Nathaniel Hawthorne, Melville wrote *Moby Dick*. His experience with *Mardi* proved prophetic for his entire career: reviews were poor and *Moby Dick* languished on the shelves. Stung, Melville attacked the book biz in his next novel, *Pierre*. HERMAN MELVILLE CRAZY! one *Pierre* review trumpeted. His reputation in decline, Melville suffered a breakdown. He recovered and other novels followed, but readers screamed, "You're finished!" After 1857 Melville published no fiction at all and only four volumes of poetry, all eminently adapted for unpopularity. His health and spirit shattered, he never again ventured into the literary marketplace. To keep his family afloat, Melville took a job for four dollars a day as a New York customs inspector. He detested the job but held it for twenty years until an inheritance enabled him to retire. When he died, his obit in the *New York Times* was only three lines long.

The story of Melville's literary rebirth is one of the strangest in the history of American literature. It began in England shortly before his death and was strong enough to give Melville hope that his work would have a place in American literature. The revival gathered steam in 1919 on the centennial of his birth. With the publication of a laudatory biography in 1921, Melville entered the ranks of the great. Melville was seen as the symbol of artistic integrity, a true artist rejected and ultimately destroyed by the petty minds of his time. This new myth was itself a distortion, but it was sufficient to catapult Melville to the major leagues. Smelling fresh critical fodder, scholars dug in the trough: from the mid-1940s to the mid-1950s, Melville mania reigned. Although Melville had burned many of his letters, and his surviving child, Frances, was so bitter against her father that she refused to speak about him, the Melville machine kept churning out biographies, critical studies, and articles. He became a pop culture icon as well: seafood restaurants, comic books, and cartoons all bore the mark of the white whale. Today his reputation is secure; Mama Melville's failure is a Big Man on Campus.

A WHALE OF A TALE

The narrator, identified only as Ishmael, decides that the sea's a fine mistress and it's time to learn more of her mysteries. Unfortunately, his first night in New Bedford, he ends up in bed with a South Seas cannibal named Queequeg. (Shame on us. The lengths to which we go to get you to read a book.)

The next day Ishmael visits the Whaleman's Chapel and hears Father Mapple deliver a stirring sermon on Jonah and the whale. The pastor exhorts the congregation to reject pride and be true to God. Ishmael and Queequeg, having hit it off just fine, board a packet boat to Nantucket in search of a whaling ship. On the brief trip, Queequeg saves an obnoxious lout from swimming with the fishies. The next day Ishmael and Queequeg sign on the *Pequod*. They hear strange rumors about Ahab, confined to his cabin by some vague illness.

The *Pequod* sails on a dreary Christmas morning. Ishmael describes the crew, including the harpooners and the three mates, Starbuck, Stubb, and Flask. As the ship enters warmer climes, Ishmael finally catches his first glimpse of Ahab, his white peg leg anchored in a hole in the deck. Ishmael describes whales and shipboard life.

WHO'S WHO

Moby Dick:
A LITERARY TOUT SHEET

Captain Ahab: Crazed one-legged hero-villain, whose defiant revenge makes him more Job's wife than Job.

Ishmael: The narrator, the Mel Gibson of sailors, compassionate, intelligent, and hunky.

Starbuck: "Bucks the stars"—the mate who fights the destiny Ahab has carved out for him.

Stubb: The average sailor, no rocket scientist but handy in a pinch.

Flask: A materialistic blockhead.

Queequeg: A huge cannibal, handy with a harpoon.

Pip: A small black man driven mad by whales and life.

Fedallah: Exorcise this demon! The harpooner who represents pure evil and badly needs orthodontia.

**WHO'S
WHO**

(Continued)

Moby Dick: One hundred feet of great white sperm whale, sushi for the masses.

The Pequod: Ahab's ship, the *QE2* from Hell.

Ahab summons the crew to the quarterdeck and tells them their mission is to hunt down the great white whale Moby Dick, who chomped off his leg during his last voyage. Ishmael finds out that Moby Dick would make a lousy house pet. Aside from his size, he has a vicious temper and eats whaleboats like Fritos.

Ahab pours over his maps, charting a course to meet Big Whitey. In the meantime, they pick up a few sperm whales along the way. On their first expedition, Ishmael finds out that Ahab has his own boat crew, East Indians led by the satanic Fedallah. The *Pequod* meets up with nine other vessels; each time Ahab tries the same light conversational gambit: "Hast seen the White Whale?" Just when you thought it was safe to go back into the water, the *Pequod* meets up with the *Samuel Enderby,* whose captain's arm made a hors d'oeuvre for Moby Dick. After a nasty typhoon, the *Pequod* meets the *Rachel,* who has just done battle with Mr. Whale. Tension mounts. Ahab sights Moby Dick!

Round 1: Moby Dick. The leviathan bites Ahab's row boat in half.

Round 2: Moby Dick. Fishy takes a bouquet of har-

FLESH AND BONE:
THE WHALING INDUSTRY

The peak years for American whaling were 1835 to 1865, when more than seven hundred vessels and seventy thousand people were whaling away. It was an industry as huge as its prey: more than five million gallons of whale oil were processed every year. The oil was used for lighting and lubricant, the bone for corset stays, the spermaceti for candles, the ambergris for perfume, and the flesh for food. The average voyage lasted three years and was rarely lucrative for the common grunt—while captains pocketed about 1/12 of the take, crew members got about 1/175 each, barely enough to cover their clothing and medicines. The discovery of petroleum in Pennsylvania in 1859 killed business, but likely saved the whales. The last American whaling vessel sailed in 1928; today the only countries with significant whaling fleets are the Russians and Japanese.

Whaling: a tough way to make a buck

P.S.: Unlike iguana, frog, and other exotic meats served in chichi French bistros, whale tastes like beef, not chicken.

poons but smashes two more boats and Fedallah is killed.

Round 3: a tie. Ahab drives a harpoon into Moby Dick, but the furious whale rams his head into the *Pequod*, crushing it. Ahab throws another harpoon into Moby Dick, but the rope catches Ahab around the neck and drags him into the inky depths. The sinking ship creates a vortex, pulling down everyone but Ishmael, who is rescued by the *Rachel*. Hey, someone has to survive to write the story.

MOCHA DICK
. . . .

In his early sailing days aboard the *Acushnet*, Melville heard tall tales about a monstrous albino whale with a scar on his forehead that the sailors dubbed "Mocha Dick" or "Moby Dick." A touchy fellow, Mr. Whale crushed whaling boats in his huge jaws, the quick and the lucky scrambling overboard in time to avoid being his dinner. The stories were based on fact: an English ship had a close encounter of the fishy kind with this whale in July of 1840; a Russian ship, a month later.

You should have seen the one that got away

IT'S A KEEPER

Don't be misled by size. *Moby Dick* is more than weighty; it's also weighted. It's an epic, a long narrative that represents characters of high position in a series of adventures of significance. Usually, an epic is unified around a central figure of heroic stature; and as a general rule, it deals with actions of great importance to a culture. *Moby Dick* is clearly a long adventure tale with great meaning, for it makes us feel deeply the dangers of pride and hatred, and evokes the inexplicable mystery of life. Ahab is an awesome character, even though we may shudder as we admire him. Symbolically, the actions have universal significance, for the story can be read as an allegory of the risks in trying to subjugate nature to the will of humanity or in rebelling against the evil and chaos in the universe. Whaling becomes a metaphor for Ishmael's search for the Meaning of Life. In addition, the story is an epic because it uses a long journey (standard epic fare), elevated language, and battles (akin to the single combats of ancient epics).

"It's Moby Dick, lads! A symbol of evil! Or perhaps death! Maybe God or, I don't know, an indifferent universe!"

THE VERY GOOD, THE VERY BAD, AND THE VERY UGLY

As *Billy Budd*, Melville's last important work opens, it's 1797 and the British merchant ship *Rights of Man* is halted at sea by the H.M.S. *Indomitable*, a man-of-war short of men but long on war. Lieutenant Ratcliffe impresses (that is, abducts) the pick of the litter, the hunky foretopman from the *Rights of Man*, Billy Budd. Amiable as well as attractive, Billy agrees to serve the King. Aboard the *Indomitable*, Billy proves a team player and popular with the assorted flotsam and jetsam of the rig. Claggart is the sole holdout; the Boss from Hell harbors an irrational hatred of the gorgeous and innocent sailor. Billy is slow on the uptake—he simply cannot fathom that someone would hate him for no reason. Dansker tries to warn Billy that Claggart is a no-goodnik, but Billy's not the swiftest kid on the block.

One night Billy is awakened by a sailor who asks him to join with some other impressed seamen in a mutiny, even throwing a few bucks his way to sweeten the pot. Enraged, Billy begins to stutter and threatens to heave the blackguard overboard. The sailor flees.

Soon after, Claggart reports to Captain Vere that Billy was trying to foment mutiny. As vicious as a mink, Claggart produces false evidence against the innocent sailor. Billy is so shocked by the charges that he cannot speak. Unable to express himself with words, Billy resorts to action, punching Claggart so hard that he kills him.

Although Vere knows that Billy had a point, he nonetheless believes it's unwise to spare the rod and spoil the child. With memories of the mutinies during the first of the Napoleonic Wars fresh in mind, Vere convenes a

WHO'S
H O 👈

Billy Budd, Foretopman:
A LITERARY TOUT SHEET

Billy Budd: A lamb in lamb's clothing—the handsome and innocent sailor hung out to dry for his goodness.

John Claggart: A wolf in wolf's clothing—the mad master-at-arms who has it in for Our Hero.

Captain Edward Fairfax "Starry" Vere: The bookish captain of the *Indomitable* who Does the Right Thing.

Dansker: The canny old salt who tries to tip off Billy to Claggart's hatred; too little, too late.

Squeak: The ratlike corporal of the lower deck who delights in carrying out Claggart's dirty work.

Lieutenant Ratcliffe: You're in the Navy now—the bluff, hearty officer who impresses Billy into naval service.

Captain Graveling: The kindly captain of the *Rights of Man.*

Officers of the Court-Martial: The anonymous representatives of blind justice. Question: Why didn't the sharks eat the lawyers who fell overboard? Answer: Professional courtesy.

**WHO'S
H
O**

☞

(Continued)

The Chaplain: The man of the cloth who likely represents Melville's belief that good and evil exist side by side.

hasty court aboard the ship. Billy is found guilty and is hanged from the yardarm the next morning. He dies with a blessing on his lips: "God bless Captain Vere!"

Soon after, the *Indomitable* encounters the *Athée* (the Atheist), a French battleship. While attempting to capture the enemy, Captain Vere is seriously hurt. The *Indomitable* wins the battle but loses the war: Vere dies soon after. On his deathbed he murmurs, "Billy Budd, Billy Budd."

Office politics being what they are, Claggart is praised as a patriotic sailor killed while carrying out his job and Billy Budd is vilified as a traitor. Nonetheless, the common sailors revere Billy as a saint and keep track of the spar from which he was hanged.

DEEP MEANING

The story is loosely based on a true incident: The *Somers* mutiny case of 1842. The attempted mutiny occurred in the American Navy aboard a small training brig, and three men were hanged. Melville's cousin, Guert Gansevoort, was the first lieutenant of the brig, so Melville had the inside scoop.

Billy Budd is a short, easy read, but you know better by now: there has to be a Deep Meaning to this simple tale of injustice. Actually, the critics have had a field day with this baby. The early critics saw the tale as embodying a sharp conflict between good and evil, personified in Billy and Claggart and finally resolved in tragic terms. Later pundits read it as a spiritual autobiography, in which Billy, Claggart, and Vere play parts corresponding, respectively, to Christ, Satan, and God. As proof, they cited Billy's cry of "God bless Captain Vere" as recalling Christ's utterance on the cross: "Father, forgive them; for they know not what they do" (Luke 23:34). To these folk, the novella was "Melville's testament of acceptance." Today a renegade sect views the story as ironic, with Billy as a passive victim of social or divine injustice. In this light, Vere is not a hero but a reactionary authoritarian; and the novella as a whole is Melville's final ironic protest against the repressive structure of society or of the cosmos itself. They read the book as "Melville's testament of resistance."

Take your pick.

LIFE BEFORE XEROX

Before the days of photocopying machines, copies were made by hand. The lucky dogs who wrote out copies were called "scriveners," a job about as interesting as watching the Home Shopping Channel. As our story opens, a successful Wall Street lawyer hires Bartleby to copy documents for his firm. For two days Bartleby is a diligent worker, and makes the A-list. But then he begins to refuse to proofread his work, and soon will not copy anything at all, politely saying, "I would prefer not to." Instead, he stares out the window at a blank wall.

"BONFIRE OF THE VANITIES"

Okay, so the City of Brotherly Love beat out the Big Apple for the first stock exchange (1791 versus 1792), but New York has Wall Street, where the sharks meet to eat. The New York Stock Exchange was established with twenty-four merchants and brokers who met under a tree at 68 Wall Street to do lunch and charge commissions while acting as agents for others. The early trading was based on government securities; later came bank and insurance stock. In 1817 the New York brokers organized formally as the New York Stock and Exchange Board, adopting the present name in 1863.

PECULIAR LITERARY MERGERS

Soon after, the lawyer discovers that Bartleby has been living at the law office. He gives the recalcitrant Bartleby time to recover from eyestrain, but when he still will not work, the lawyer is forced to pull the plug. To his astonishment, Bartleby refuses to leave. Unable to dislodge Bartleby, the lawyer moves his practice to another building, leaving Bartleby behind in the deserted offices. The new tenants, outraged at the uninvited squatter, have Bartleby arrested for vagrancy and sent to a prison called the "Tombs."

The lawyer visits the Tombs and finds that Bartleby is

WHO'S
H
O ☞

"Bartleby, the Scrivener":
A LITERARY TOUT SHEET

Bartleby: The copyist in a law office who suddenly and inexplicably refuses to work, move, or respond. Like the person sitting next to you on the subway last Tuesday. And this Tuesday.

The Lawyer: The complacent narrator of the story, a sixtyish lawyer who learns compassion when reality won't bend to his will.

Ginger Nut: Twelve-year-old office gofer with an appetite for ginger nuts.

Nippers: Maalox king who does his best copying *after* lunch.

Turkey: Candidate for Richard Simmons who does his best copying *before* lunch.

staring at the wall, although he is free to roam the prison yard. Upon his next visit, he finds Bartleby's huddled form lying dead at the base of a wall. The lawyer later hears that Bartleby was forced out of a job at the Dead Letter Office. He feels enormous pity for Bartleby and all of humankind. Okay, so it's sort of a downer; Melville's life was no bed of petunias, you know.

GOOD HELP IS HARD TO FIND

The story can be read as a parable of walls, showing how the world of commerce, symbolized by Wall Street, stifles the human spirit. Imprisoned in an emotional ghetto by physical barriers (the city's walls) and emotional ones (a job devoid of meaning), Bartleby represents a misspent life. He's the original Dead End Kid, trapped in the Dead Letter Office of life.

Early critics of the story gleefully pointed out parallels between Melville and his fictional creation, since both were discarded artists "walled in" by an unappreciative public. The public recoiled in horror when Melville attempted to write something more meaningful than a titillating travelogue; the lawyer was nonplussed when Bartleby didn't want to be a human Xerox.

Typee

In the summer of 1842, the narrator, a young sailor named Tom, jumps ship at Nukuheva Island, one of the three islands in the Marquesas. Toby, an equally disgruntled fellow sailor, agrees to come along for the ride. The sailors end up in paradise, Typee Valley.

Baywatch, 1845.
The South Seas; the idyllic setting for Typee.

Welcomed by Mehevi, the chief of the Typees, Tom and Toby are feted and entertained by native cheerleader types. Tommo, as the natives call him, and his sore leg are treated with special tenderness by the nubile young Fayaway. He learns how the Nukuhevans make tapa cloth as well as whoopie, but refuses to be tattooed. Toby goes off to find medical treatment for Tom's leg and vanishes. Tom begins to realize that he's stumbled into a Hotel California, not Club Med: you can check out anytime you want, but you can never leave.

Paradise becomes Purgatory when Tommo interrupts the cheerful, gentle Typees admiring three disembodied human heads. Warriors go off to battle an enemy tribe, the Happars. Upon their return, the tribe enjoys a little nosh on the bloody remains. Terrified that he's slated to be the Happy Meal, Tommo makes a break for an

English whaleboat in the harbor. He later learns that the captain of the whaleboat had masterminded his escape and was arranging to barter for his release. In "The Story of Toby," a sequel, we learn that Toby is also taken off the island by a passing ship and has returned home safely.

Typee, the first great romance about the South Seas, represents Melville's search for a primitive society that could preserve the values that civilization had lost. Tommo, a twentieth-century Adam seeking a nineteenth-century paradise, blunders into an unspoiled Eden, a land free of cynicism and social prejudice. Okay, so there's a little cannibalism, but hey, no place is perfect.

SUMMARY

⏱ Created America's greatest prose epic, *Moby Dick*, and is ranked as one of America's greatest novelists.

⏱ Fashioned the first great romance about the South Seas.

⏱ Lent his whale imagery to countless fish joints.

Emily Dickinson, 1830-1886,
American poet and recluse nonpareil

CHAPTER 10

EMILY DICKINSON
(1830–1886)

YOU MUST REMEMBER THIS

Dickinson is revered for the concrete imagery, forceful language, and unique style of her 1,775 poems.

MOST FAMOUS FOR

Giving agoraphobia a good name; making the Phantom of the Opera look like a party animal. Founding mother of American poetry.

254

"Hope" is the thing with feathers—
That perches in the soul—
And sings the tune without the words—
And never stops—at all—

WITHOUT FEATHERS

Born to the upper crust of Amherst, Massachusetts, Dickinson seemed to get the crumbs. Her grandfather founded Amherst College; her father was that rare species, a well-respected lawyer. The bloodline was a little watered down by the time brother Austin arrived, but he was a looker and his wife a social climber of first order. Sister Lavinia, while not a rocket scientist, did have the common sense to ignore Emily's instructions in her will to destroy her poems. Instead, she displayed an admirable fanaticism about having them published. And then there was Emily.

When not grinding away at chemistry, theology, Greek, Latin, ancient history, and other equally frivolous subjects, Emily enjoyed quiet reading clubs, outdoor jaunts, and socials. At fifteen she displayed typical adolescent modesty when she wrote, "I am growing very handsome very fast indeed! I expect to be the belle of Amherst when I reach my 17th year. I don't doubt that I shall have perfect crowds of admirers at that age." She may have been a hell of a poet, but she was no prophet. After she put in a two-year stint at Mount Holyoke Female Seminary, a new women's college, her social life began to narrow. For a few years she enjoyed concerts, lectures, and parties, and in 1855 she took a trip to Philadelphia and Washington, D.C., the longest journey she took in her life. But by the end of the decade, the Belle of Amherst became its most famous recluse.

Some theorize that a thwarted love affair with the Reverend Charles Wadsworth sent Emily into her room; others attribute her isolation to a deep depression. According to current feminist theory, Emily chose to live deliberately, simply, and alone, à la Thoreau. Regardless of the cause, Emily shut herself into her room, declining all visitors, dressing only in white, and after 1872, rarely leaving her room, never her house. She communicated with people mainly through mysterious notes and fragments of poems. With so much time on her hands, Emily wrote . . . and wrote . . . and wrote. No literary anorexia here: during her fifty-five years, she wrote 1,775 poems and numerous fragments. But she published only seven poems during her lifetime, all anonymously, but not for lack of effort. Her poems did not rhyme, her tribulations had no meter, her figurative language was

THE WEAKER SEX

Auntie Em was hanging by her fingernails, but this was nothing unusual for women of her class. Between 1865 and 1920, class differences between women (and men, for that matter) were especially sharp, and the lifestyle of upper-class ladies had little in common with that of working-class drudges. The latter were expected to toil at backbreaking jobs, but affluent women were considered too delicate for any exertion. Such women were often diagnosed with "nervous disorders," and the most well-heeled were subject to Dr. S. Mitchell Weir's famed "rest cure." Isolation, rest, and warm baths were the cornerstones of this treatment. Forbidden spicy food, women were fed milk, puddings, and cereals. No visitors, work, and "mental excitement" were allowed. Hmmm . . . now that we think about it, that doesn't sound half-bad. Where do we sign up?

too striking. Dickinson amassed a huge collection of reject notices.

As facts have given way to factoids, conversation to sound bites, so Dickinson has had to wait until the twentieth century to be appreciated. It wasn't until her complete poems were published in 1955 that she received a full critical appraisal. Why? Check out the following two examples:

Nineteenth-Century Poetic Style	Twentieth-Century Poetic Style
"A Tender Lay"	**956**
Be gentle to the new laid egg,	What shall I do when the Summer troubles—
For eggs are brilliant things;	What, when the Rose is ripe—
They cannot fly until they're hatched,	What when the Eggs fly off in Music
And have a pair of wings.	From the Maple Keep?

The anonymous poem on the left was a bestseller in 1857; Emily's version of the same theme, which appears on the right, was unpublished in her lifetime. First problem: Dickinson's poems don't *look* like poems are supposed to look. Where are the commas, semicolons, and periods? What about conventional sentence structure? Everyone in the nineteenth century knew that good poetry had to rhyme. And then we have the ideas. Aren't poems supposed to sound like Mother's Day cards, all warm and fuzzy? Dickinson avoided the sticky sentimentality of popular nineteenth-century poetry, favoring instead startling images and outlooks. Her poems paved the way for the

Imagist movement of the 1920s and she became one of the movement's patron saints. As you can imagine, this made Dickinson's poems very unpopular with her contemporaries.

When Dickinson died, her sister discovered piles of poems, many bound into neat little booklets. She brought the poems to a neighbor, Mabel Loomis Todd, also a writer, who arranged to have the poems published with the help of the well-known critic Thomas Wentworth Higginson. Todd and Higginson cut apart the little booklets and rearranged the poems into the conventional poetic topics of the time: Love,

---

IMAGISM

Ezra Pound, 1885-1972, American avant-garde poet, critic, translator, and traitor

As sleek and stripped down as Sharon Stone, Imagism hawked radical and original images and hard truths. Shunning rhythm and rhyme, the Imagists depended on the power of the image itself to arrest attention and convey emotion. Founded by jut-jawed Amy Lowell in 1912, the torch was carried by acolytes Hilda Doolittle (H. D.), Ezra Pound, and William Carlos Williams. Here's a classic imagist poem by Ezra Pound, who penned some nifty stuff when he wasn't busy being a traitor:

In a Station of the Metro
The apparition of these faces in the crowd;
Petals on a wet, black bough.

(1913)

Nature, Friendship, Death, Immortality, and so on. The book was a smash: it was reprinted twice in two months and ran into eleven editions within two years. When critics complained that Dickinson was inept and unskilled, various editors revised her poems to appeal more to conventional taste: words were changed, lines revised, conventional punctuation substituted for the dashes. Slowly, over the years, different editors returned the poems to their original state and proper order. The 1955 complete edition arranged the poems in the order in which they had been found, as much as possible, and used numbers in place of the titles Todd and others had slapped on. The dashes, which varied in length and angle, were restored and edited punctuation deleted. The complete philosophical and tragic dimensions of Dickinson's vision then became apparent, and her poems could then be fully appreciated. Let's look at some of her most famous poems.

249

Wild Nights—Wild Nights!
Were I with thee
Wild Nights should be
Our luxury!

Futile—the Winds—
To a Heart in port—
Done with the Compass—
Done with the Chart!

Rowing in Eden—
Ah, the Sea!
Might I but moor—Tonight—
In Thee!

REMEMBRANCE OF FLINGS PAST?

This brief yearning for reunion with a lover is a shocker:
Is this the recluse who rejected Love for Art? The sexual
imagery is astonishingly explicit for a woman not known
for going out walkin' after midnight. The speaker fanta-
sizes about X-rated nights when the lovers are reunited.
Just to make sure that we don't misread her intentions,
the poet repeated "Wild Nights" twice and adds an ex-
clamation point. The "port" in stanza 2 and the "moor"
in stanza 3 are clear sexual images.

Beginning with the unusual rhyme scheme a-b-b-b
(nights, thee, be, luxury), the poem abandons rhyme in
the second stanza, then picks it up again at the end. The
varying rhythms, unusual for Dickinson's work, serve to
convey the depths of the lover's anguish. The speaker
must be in hell if she can't even keep her meter regular.
A startling analogy such as comparing making whoopee
with sailing is characteristic of the metaphysical poetry
of the seventeenth century. Puritans Edward Taylor and
Anne Bradstreet brought this style of poetry to the New
World; Dickinson was familiar with both their work.

One of the most hotly debated topics among academics is Dickinson's sex life, which shows you how exciting
it is to be a professor. One camp holds that Dickinson
fell in love with the married clergyman Charles Wads-

worth when he was forty and she twenty-three. In 1862 Wadsworth left the City of Brotherly Love for the Golden State of California. According to tradition, Dickinson was shattered and turned to poetry for consolation. It is more certain that Dickinson fell passionately in love with Judge Otis P. Lord near the end of her life.

Whatever happened behind Emily's closed door, few poems have captured the power of anticipated love as strongly as this one. The reference to the Garden of Eden in the last stanza suggests that even if love cannot return people to Paradise, it does offer sanctuary to exiles.

986

A narrow Fellow in the Grass
Occasionally rides—
You may have met Him—did you not
His notice sudden is—

The Grass divides as with a Comb—
A spotted shaft is seen—
And then it closes at your feet
And opens further on—

He likes a Boggy Acre
A Floor to cool for Corn—
Yet when a Boy, and Barefoot—
I more than once at Noon
Have passed, I thought, a Whip lash
Upbraiding in the Sun
When stooping to secure it
It wrinkled, and was gone—

Several of Nature's People
I know, and they know me—
I feel for them a transport
Of cordiality—

But never met this Fellow
Attended, or alone
Without a tighter breathing
And Zero at the Bone—

A SNAKE IN THE GRASS

Like many literary lights, Dickinson is easier to reread than to read. At first glance, this poem looks like free verse, but the underlying metrical structure incorporates the traditional patterns of English hymns, alternating lines of eight and six syllables. The tone is deceptively light and simple—First Date Cool—as we meet that affable fellow, Mr. Snake. The language, however, assaults

A snake in the grass

the reader as much as the encounter with the snake. The inversion in the lines "You may have met Him— did you not/His notice sudden is—" jerks language from its everyday function just as the snake has jerked the speaker from feeling at home in nature. Dickinson's ability to use language to reflect experience marks her as one of the first modern poets.

The metaphors used to describe Mr. Snake reflect the speaker's changing feelings about it. The reptile goes from being a civilized "Fellow" to a vaguely ominous "spotted shaft" to a definitely hostile "Whip lash" to an openly evil "it." Like the giant carrot James Arness becomes in the frozen north, the snake engenders terror, "tighter breathing/And Zero at the Bone—" The serpentine lines and repeated *s* sounds of the beginning give way to the *o* of terror—fell*ow*, al*o*ne, zer*o*, b*o*ne.

The poem describes a journey into the heart of nature's darkness, a major theme in American Literature. It begins with Emerson's view of nature as a groovy way to channel wholeness, but we soon find out that nature is really more like *Nightmare on Elm Street.* Nature toys with people, often unraveling their grip on reality. The "Whip lash" shows us that nature wears hip boots and lots of leather.

712

Because I could not stop for Death—
He kindly stopped for me—
The Carriage held but just Ourselves—
And Immortality.

We slowly drove—He knew no haste
And I had put away
My labor and my leisure too,
For His Civility—

We passed the School, where Children strove
At Recess—in the Ring—
We passed the Fields of Gazing Grain—
We passed the Setting Sun—

Or rather—He passed Us—
The Dews drew quivering and chill—
For only Gossamer, my Gown—
My Tippet—only Tulle—

We paused before a House that seemed
A Swelling in the Ground—
The Roof was scarcely visible—
The Cornice—in the Ground—

Since then—'tis Centuries—and yet
Feels shorter than the Day
I first surmised the Horses' Heads
Were toward Eternity—

A DATE WITH DESTINY

A hot date turns out to be an encounter with that old charmer, Death. Because the speaker is too busy to stop and die, Death stops by in his limo. He brings along Immortality as a chaperon. Only after Death has the speaker in his nasty embrace does she see that Death makes a lousy date. The ghoulish seducer of her poem

LITSPEAK CRIB SHEET
Here's a sampling of lit lingo:

Allegory: A literary work with two levels of meaning, one literal and the rest symbolic. John Bunyan's *Pilgrim's Progress* is a hot example.

Free verse: Poetry without a regular rhyme or rhythm. Uncle Walt did it first.

Gothic: The Bates mansion and its contents. Wild, mysterious literary elements.

Metaphor: A comparison. Successful ones use language in vivid and imaginative ways; flops become clichés favored by your Aunt Agnes.

Meter: In literature, a poem's rhythmical pattern; in life, an odd-shaped device that demands quarters on a regular basis.

Simile: A comparison that uses "like" or "as."

Personification: A figure of speech in which a nonhuman subject is given human qualities. Frankenstein with a twist.

Rhyme: The repetition of sounds at the end of words. Rhyming the last lines of poems creates "end rhyme"; rhyming words in the middle of lines creates "internal rhyme." Except for Hallmark cards, rhyme is as out as John Denver, Crisco, and Hamburger Helper.

Rhythm: The pattern of beats, or stresses, in language. Traditional poetry follows a regular rhythmical pattern; modern poetry does not.

would be right at home in any nineteenth-century Gothic novel.

Death seduces the speaker with his smoothness. The poem shows us how close death is, even though we never realize it. As a result, people are caught unprepared when Death comes a-calling. The compression of words and ideas in stanza 3 demonstrates this. This stanza traces the cycle of life, from childhood (the School) to death (the Setting Sun). Time marches on, even for children—and even though its pace seems to crawl when we're young. The word "passed" in the same stanza shows the irony of this: the occupants of the carriage are not only passing some scenes, they are also passing out of life. The disheveled rhyme scheme, alternating iambic tetrameter and trimeter lines, underscores our unpreparedness for death.

Death is Auntie Em's favorite theme. No doubt this was partly because thirty-three of her friends and family died between 1851 and 1854 alone. The moral: Life is short and death is long. So call your mother already.

214

I taste a liquor never brewed—
From Tankards scooped in Pearl—
Not all the Vats upon the Rhine
Yield such an Alcohol!

Inebriate of Air—am I—
And Debauchee of Dew—
Reeling—thro endless summer days—
From inns of Molten Blue—

When "Landlords" turn the drunken Bee
Out of the Foxglove's door—
When Butterflies—renounce their "drams"—
I shall but drink the more!

Till Seraphs swing their snowy Hats—
And Saints—to windows run—
To see the little Tippler
Leaning against the—Sun—

BOTTOMS UP!

In this poem Emily compares the exhilaration of going
outside in summer to the buzz of getting drunk in a bar.
We can safely assume the second half of the comparison
is not based on Em's personal experience. Maybe not
even the first half.

Anyway, the poem trods as carefully as any drunk.
The pauses and repetition break up the otherwise uni-
form marching rhythm to suggest staggering—of the
drunk losing physical control and of the poet stumbling into divinity. In stanza 3, the flower becomes the
bee's tavern. The reference to "Landlords" turning
out the "drunken Bee" recalls the temperance movement, one of the hot topics of the time. Dickinson
uses the reference to poke fun at the earnest WASP
approach to temperance. In the final stanza, her
drunken staggering calls forth angels and saints. The
speaker is not leaning on the lamppost, as we would
expect, but against the sun itself, the visible symbol
of holiness.

Here we see one of the main themes of Dickinson's
poetry, the religious quest, a desire to know the Purpose

Tour # 164
All Inclusive Five Day Tour

Itinerary For: *Emily Dickinson*

<u>MONDAY</u>: Visit to the Kitchen. Ideally located with bathroom on one side and a magnificent view of the lawn on the other side.

<u>TUESDAY</u>: Visit to the Garden Gate. An oasis of full range greenery, afternoon sun and romantic gazebo.

<u>WEDNESDAY</u>: Visit to the Study. View the lovely booklined walls, ornate drapery, comfortable seating and indirect candle lighting.

<u>THURSDAY</u>: Visit to the Bedroom. Overlook lush garden greenery. Admire the quaint wallpaper, 17th century charm, sumptuous footbath and one appropriately sized closet. Marvel at the handcrafted dresser adorned with a doily. Study your reflection in the sparkling framed mirror.

<u>FRIDAY</u>: Visit to the Porch. Sumptuous cool breezes and a magnificent wooden archway are just two of the unique features that await you.

All inclusive features include daily breakfast, lunch and dinner, plus day-time snacks and all baggage handling.
<u>*Upgrade Available:*</u> *Larger outside bedroom on higher level.*

A. BACALL

of Life. By drawing on her own experience to answer these questions, she allies herself with the Romantic poets, who gave primary authority to personal experience rather than book learnin'. "I taste a liquor never brewed" captures a moment of certainty when Dickinson believed that this world was a highway to heaven. Many of her other poems paint hell on earth, and depict life as an activity about as useful as rearranging the deck chairs on the *Titanic*.

465

I heard a Fly buzz—when I died—
The Stillness in the Room
Was like the Stillness in the Air—
Between the Heaves of Storm—

The Eyes around—has wrung them dry—
And Breaths were gathering firm
For that last Onset—when the King
Be witnessed—in the Room—

I willed my Keepsakes—Signed away
What portion of me be
Assignable—and then it was
There interposed a Fly—

With Blue—uncertain stumbling Buzz—
Between the light—and me—
And then the Windows failed—and then
I could not see to see—

THE FLY

Another of Emily's tales from the crypt, this poem describes the events leading up to the speaker's death. The
first stanza describes the quiet room; the second, the
bedside deathwatch. The little visitor who strafes the
third stanza is a symbol for Beelzebub, lord of the flies
and king of the devils. For a believer, the symbol is horri-
fying: it suggests that the soul dies with the body.

  As with her better-known contemporaries, Emerson,
Hawthorne, Melville, and Thoreau, Dickinson was deeply

concerned about conventional Christianity and death. Dickinson creates the moment of death to find an instant of clarity, but instead of angels and choirs, we get a fly. Death ends the illumination and plunges the speaker into darkness. What does the fly represent? Death? Hell? God? The fly points the way, but the living cannot interpret its buzz, and the voice stops.

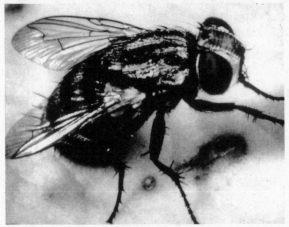

"Cecile! Cecile!"

LORD OF THE FLIES

William Golding cashed some hefty checks for his 1954 allegory of good and evil, *Lord of the Flies*. A nasty *Swiss Family Robinson*, the novel traces how a group of British schoolboys revert to savagery when shipwrecked on a remote Pacific island. Marianne Wiggins (Salman Rushdie's ex) did the feminist version in the late 1980s—*John Dollar*, which describes how a group of girls become savages. This is why parents stock the house with chips, hire babysitters, and leave no telephone number.

GETTING THE LAST WORD

So what do famous people say when they shuffle off this mortal coil? Comedian W. C. Fields said, "All things considered, I'd rather be in Philadelphia." The near-dead have more time to think. As Woody Allen said, "I'm not afraid to die. I just don't want to be there when it happens." According to Johnny Carson, "For three days after death, hair and fingernails continue to grow but phone calls taper off."

SUMMARY

⏱ Was the founding mother of American poetry. Her rich visual imagery, unique style, and unusual metaphors paved the way for modern poetry.

⏱ Plumbed philosophical and tragic dimensions of life.

⏱ Set up the first home office with a vengeance.

Samuel Langhorne Clemens (Mark Twain), 1835-1910,
American writer and humorist

CHAPTER 11

MARK TWAIN

(1835–1910)

YOU MUST REMEMBER THIS

Mark Twain (the pen name of Samuel Langhorne Clemens) rocketed to fame with humorous local-color tales of the West; he became a media darling by transforming stories of his childhood into American myth. Ernest Hemingway, a famous dead guy, claimed, "All modern American literature comes from one book by Mark Twain called *Huckleberry Finn*." Although we now know that Hemingway was an insensitive macho pig, we are willing to admit that he was right about Twain.

MOST FAMOUS FOR

His pen name, Mark Twain, the Mississippi riverboat code for "safe water." Also created a literary language based on colloquial American speech that put him in front of the pack as the greatest American writer. Twain's most famous works are:

- ★ "The Celebrated Jumping Frog of Calaveras County" (1865)
- ★ *The Innocents Abroad* (1869)
- ★ *Roughing It* (1872)
- ★ *The Adventures of Tom Sawyer* (1876)
- ★ *The Prince and the Pauper* (1882)
- ★ *Life on the Mississippi* (1883)
- ★ *The Adventures of Huckleberry Finn* (1884)
- ★ *A Connecticut Yankee in King Arthur's Court* (1889)
- ★ "The Man That Corrupted Hadleyburg" (1900)
- ★ *The Mysterious Stranger* (1916)

THE ABRAHAM LINCOLN OF
AMERICAN LITERATURE

It's brutally hard to write a bio on Twain because the man was so damned blameless. Saint Sam was a vocal champion of any oppressed minority: slave or free, male or female, domestic or foreign, animal, mineral, or vegetable. He campaigned for black rights, supported workers, and deplored anti-Semitism. Amazing for his day, he supported Native Americans with a zeal that would have impressed Marlon Brando. Even though he suffered from a bad case of chivalry, gallantry, and all the other virtues we now know are really vices in disguise, he always spoke out in favor of women. He was devoted to his invalid wife and famously tender to his daughters. Okay, he smoked foul cigars and liked a beer or two. That's all we could dig up on him. So fire us.

Born in Missouri, Samuel Langhorne Clemens grew up in the river town of Hannibal, the backwoods heaven and hell of his most famous novels. Sam's father died when the boy was twelve, and from then on he toiled to support himself and the rest of his large family. As many have noted, the brevity of Twain's boyhood may have made him value it all the more. Apprenticed to a printer, Twain learned the trade thoroughly, but soon headed west. At twenty-one he circled back home and learned to pilot a Mississippi riverboat, a prestigious and well-paying career. When the Civil War put the kibosh on river trade, Twain tried a series of get-rich schemes that got him poor fast. Scraping bottom, he turned to his pen. Writing under the pseudonym "Mark Twain," Clemens cut his literary teeth on newspaper features.

Twain had no plans for a literary career, not even a

Mississippi River, setting for Twain's most famous novels

ONLY THE NAME IS CHANGED
TO PROTECT THE INNOCENT

In taking a pen name, Clemens was going with the literary flow. His mentor, Charles Farrar Browne (1834–1867), wrote as "Artemus Ward"; fellow frontier humorists included "Petroleum Vesuvius Nasby" (David Ross Locke), "Orpheus C. Kerr" (Robert Henry Newell), and "Josh Billings" (Henry Wheeler Shaw). Other famous pen names include "Boz," (Charles Dickens), "Lewis Carroll" (Charles Lutwidge Dodgson), "George Eliot" (Mary Ann Evans), "O. Henry" (William Sydney Porter), "George Orwell" (Eric Blair), "Voltaire" (François-Marie Arouet), and "Woody Allen" (Allen Stewart Konigsberg).

permanent home, but that quickly changed. First came the Good Woman. Twain wooed and won Olivia Langdon, the delicate daughter of a New York Daddy Warbucks. For years, the conventional wisdom was that Livy, Our Lady of the Slipcover, reduced the swaggering, swearing man's man to a New Age weenie. Livy never did break Twain of his habits of keeping himself healthy with copious and frequent doses of whiskey, wearing flamboyant white suits in defiance of the universal Victorian black broadcloth, and perpetually telling bawdy stories in a frontier drawl. Nonetheless, a closer look shows the marriage was remarkably happy for both partners. In terms of the family's finances, *The Innocents Abroad* brought their ship in and *Life on the Mississippi* docked it. Since mass wants class, Twain bought the manor to which he wasn't born, a tasteful little spread in Connecticut. Forty years of fame and fortune followed.

By the 1890s, however, Twain's life was in a shambles. His health broken, his fortune lost in the Panic of 1893, his favorite daughter dead of meningitis, Twain plunged into a fresh hell. Although deeply embittered, he continued to write and lecture. Twain was extraordinarily popular on the lecture circuit, a popular venue for public entertainment before movies, TV, radio, and Ross Perot. Twain died as he had been born, in a year when Haley's comet soared overhead.

Twain in his later years

WHO'S
H
O ☞

"The Celebrated Jumping Frog of Calaveras County":
A LITERARY TOUT SHEET

Simon Wheeler: As windy as Chicago; a blowhard whose blathering stirs up a yen for Aunt Martha's whining about her root canal.

Jim Smiley: Hapless candidate for Gamblers Anonymous.

The Narrator: Name withheld to protect the innocent.

Dan'l Webster: Kermit of Calaveras County.

The unnamed narrator, a stranger in town, calls on Simon Wheeler to inquire about the friend of a friend, one Leonidas W. Smiley. The narrator soon learns that his friend has set him up: there is no Leonidas Smiley. Wheeler backs the narrator into a corner and launches into the table of one Jim Smiley, whose love of gambling is rivaled only by Imelda Marcos's shoe fetish.

Smiley will bet on anything. When Parson Walker's wife seems to be recovering from an illness, for example, Smiley says he'll risk "two-and-a-half" that her improvement is only temporary. In true tall-tale fashion, Smiley's bets stretch the reader's credulity. Smiley is especially proud of his "fifteen-minute nag," who always cavorts to the finish line first, despite her asthmatic wheezing. Smiley delights in conning the spectators into giving the nag a two hundred-yard start, but the poor glue-factory reject could "always fetch up at the stand just about a neck ahead, as near as you could cipher it down," as Wheeler tells the narrator. In the same way, Smiley's ornery bull pup, named Andrew Jackson after the tenacious President, always manages to win dog fights. The little dog waits until the last minute to grab onto an opponent's hind leg to

> "grip and hang on till they threw up the sponge, if it was a year. Smiley always come out a winner on that pup, till he harnessed a dog once that didn't have no hind legs, because they'd been sawed off by a circular saw, and when the thing had gone along far enough, and the money was all up, and he come to make a snatch for his pet holt, he saw in a minute how he'd been imposed on, and how the other dog had him in the door, so to speak, and he 'peared surprised, and then he looked sorter discouraged-like, and didn't try no more to win the fight, and so he got shucked out bad. He give Smiley a look, as much to say his heart was broke and it was *his* fault, for putting up a dog that hadn't no hind legs for him to take holt of, which was his main dependence in a fight, and then he limped off a piece and laid down and died. It was a good pup, was that Andrew Jackson, and would have made a name for hisself if he'd lived, for the stuff was in him and he had genius . . ."

Soon after, Smiley "ketched a frog one day, and took him home, and said he cal'lated to edurcate him; so he never done nothing for three months but set in his back yard and learn that frog to jump." Dan'l Webster, the talented frog named after the silver-tongued orator and diplomat, learns his lessons well and captures the admiration of the local frog fanciers. One day the proverbial stranger strolls into town and Smiley sets him up for the kill. The stranger deliberately taunts Smiley—"Well, I don't see no p'ints [points] about that frog that's any better'n any other frog"—and Smiley, hooked, bets $40 that Dan'l can outjump any other frog in Calaveras County. Smiley, no rocket scientist, leaves Dan'l with the stranger while he goes off to the swamp to fetch an amphibious opponent. The stranger debates a moment and then fills Dan'l up with quail shot, small lead pellets. Smiley returns with a choice specimen and the race begins. Dan'l "give a heave, and hysted up his shoulders—so—like a Frenchman, but it warn't no use—he couldn't budge; he was planted as solid as a church." The stranger's frog wins and hops off with a smile; the stranger gets the pot.

DANIEL WEBSTER (1782–1852)

He may have looked like a frog, but he sure didn't sound like one. Famed for his oratorical skills, lawyer Webster was no ambulance chaser. Aside from winning several famous constitutional cases in front of the Supreme Court, Webster was elected to the House of Representatives (1813) and the Senate (1827) and appointed Secretary of State (1841). His silvery tongue became the stuff of literary as well as popular legend when Stephen Vincent Benét had him outtalk the devil in the 1937 short story "The Devil and Daniel Webster."

Baffled, Smiley turns over the baggy frog, who promptly belches out a double handful of shot. Smiley sets after the stranger—and his $40—but never sees either again.

Here Simon Wheeler is interrupted in his recital, and the grateful narrator attempts a hasty retreat. Simon buttonholes the beleaguered man with a new tale of a "yaller [yellow] one-eyed cow that didn't have no tail, only a short stump like a bannanner and—" but the stranger makes good his escape.

THE TALL TALE
. . . .
The tall tale began as an oral tradition that involved travelers and settlers swapping exaggerated stories over campfires. Legendary subjects included folk heroes John Henry, Mike Fink, and Paul Bunyan. Each yarn-spinner tried to top the last outrageous stretcher during the long, lonely frontier nights. The tradition survives, in condensed form, in the self-descriptions you find in the personal ads.

WHAT ABOUT THE ONE
THAT GOT AWAY?

According to one of Twain's biographers, Our Man in the West first heard the story that would become "The Jumping Frog" in a barroom of a rundown tavern in Angel's Camp, California, while he was prospecting for gold. What he was doing prospecting for gold in a tavern we'll never know, but Twain *did* find gold in this gem of a tale. The original storyteller was "a solemn, fat-witted person, who dozed by the stove, or told slow, endless stories, without point or application.'' Twain based many of his stories on tall tales he had heard in bars, on the trail, or around campfires. This is why the IRS invented the business deduction.

Critics agree that ''The Jumping Frog'' is likely the best humorous sketch America has produced. Twain, as with many of the American West's funnymen, created humor by relating wildly exaggerated stories in a dead-pan tone, which underscores the humor because it implies that the narrator is unaware of the absurdity of the story. Twain wasn't the first writer to combine high style with low, nor the first to squander highfalutin genius on a shaggy-frog story. What was new, electric, and instantly popular was the quality of the story that resulted when he switched from standard written English to the vernacular. Every subsequent humor writer, from James Thurber to S.J. Perelman to Woody Allen, labors in Twain's shadow.

HUCK AND JIM'S EXCELLENT ADVENTURE

Here's how the novel starts:

> You don't know about me without you have read a book by the name of *The Adventures of Tom Sawyer*, but that ain't no matter. That book was made by Mr. Mark Twain and he told the truth, mainly. There was things that he stretched, but mainly he told the truth. That is nothing. I never seen nobody but lied one time or another, without it was Aunt

Polly, or the widow, maybe Mary. Aunt Polly—Tom's Aunt Polly, she is—and Mary and the Widow Douglas is all told about in that book, which is mostly a true book; some stretchers as I said before.

The Widow Douglas and her sister Miss Watson are hell-bent on cleaning up the swearing, smoking Huck. To that end, they force him to go to school, sleep in a bed, and wear clean clothes. Huck slowly adjusts to "sivilization" until he finds footprints that reveal that his no-account father is back to seize the $6,000 in robbers' treasure that Huck and Tom found in a cave. With a quick-minded caginess that would make a Swiss banker blush, Huck quickly signs the money over to Judge Thatcher.

Furious that he can't get his hands on the windfall, Pap abducts Huck and locks him in an isolated cabin. What follows is a scene that would make Stephen King's blood run cold: Pap beats the child bloody and tries to starve him into submission. Huck finally escapes by faking his own death. He kills a pig and festoons the cabin with its blood. The boy lands on Jackson's Island to hide until the excitement blows over.

Three days later Huck discovers Jim, Miss Watson's black slave, who has run away because Miss Watson wants to sell him down the river. Although horrified that Jim would try to escape, Huck swears to keep his secret. Fearing capture, the dynamic duo raft down the Mississippi, planning to hop a steamboat and travel to Ohio, a free state. Huck becomes embroiled in a fictional version of the Hatfield and McCoy feud when the Grangerfords and the Shepherdsons shoot it out over an issue neither can remember. A little farther on, our heroes are suckered by two con men pretending to be royalty. These

**WHO'S
H
O** ☞

The Adventures of Huckleberry Finn:
A LITERARY TOUT SHEET

Huckleberry Finn: Dennis the Menace Home Alone on the frontier: the self-reliant, mischievous, thoughtful boy you wish you had been but wouldn't babysit for if they paid you in six-packs.

Tom Sawyer: The guy who taps the keg, wears the toga, and still manages to ace physics. Boys will be boys.

Jim: The black man whose only mistake was being born a Southern slave.

Pap, Huck's father: Father in name only, a drunken bundle of poor white trash who proves that the twentieth century doesn't have a lock on child abuse.

The Duke and the King: Nineteenth-century con men who are one sandwich short of a picnic.

The Grangerfords and the Shepherdsons: And the feud goes on; Twain's version of the Hatfields and the McCoys.

The Mississippi: A state of mind as much as a body of water; Old Man River represents freedom and unifies the action.

guys are male versions of the Queen of Mean, and they happily cheat their way downriver. With all this action, the raft misses the turnoff at Cairo and heads deeper into slave territory.

After a violent tussle with his conscience, Huck decides to help Jim escape from slavery. The plot goes down for the count when Huck and Jim arrive at the Phelps farm, the home of Tom's Aunt Polly. Huck is mistaken for Tom Sawyer, Tom for Sid Sawyer, and Tom contrives an elaborate scheme for Jim's escape. When the scheme fails and Tom is shot in the leg, the scamp finally admits that Jim has been free all along, thanks to Miss Watson's timely death and humane will. Jim tells Huck that Pap has died; Huck decides that writing is too much trouble and heads off. ''There ain't nothing more to write about,'' he concludes, ''and I am rotten glad of it, because if I'd a knowed what a trouble it was to make a book I wouldn't a tackled it and ain't agoing to no more. But I reckon I

THE TOM SAWYER OF TIMES SQUARE

got to light out for the Territory ahead of the rest, because Aunt Sally she's going to adopt me and sivilize me and I can't stand it. I been there before.''

PC OR NOT PC

The federal government once asked a committee of English teachers to prepare a list of books that should be required reading for all students. They could agree unanimously on only one book—*The Adventures of Huckleberry Finn*. Nonetheless, you should read the book.

Huck Finn is the book that created American Literature. Twain's mythic tale of death and rebirth and freedom and bondage uses the metaphor of slavery as a metaphor for all social bondage and institutionalized injustice and inhumanity. Jim's search for freedom and Huck's need to escape his mothering-figures is as much a symbolic search for freedom as it is a flight from slavery to sanctuary. Freedom exists on the raft and river, not in the North or in the South.

The two major targets of Twain's wit are institutionalized religion and the romanticism of the South. The first is shown by the Widow's hypocritical attempts to teach Huck about religion while she owns slaves. Huck's decision to free Jim makes him more ''religious'' than the Widow and everyone else around him. The senseless feud epitomizes the South's mindless adherence to the myths of its past, its reliance on form over substance.

Beneath the uproarious comedy of the novel, there is a tragic view of the Garden of Eden, one of the great visions of the unattainable world of the Noble Savage,

Western civ's perennial secular dream of salvation.
The theme started in American Lit with our first Wild
Man, James Fenimore Cooper's Natty Bumppo. In the

ERNEST HEMINGWAY (1899–1961)

*Ernest Hemingway, 1899-1961,
macho novlist, reporter, and
sportsman*

Sherwood Anderson, William Faulkner, and Ernest Hemingway all labored in the shadow of Twain's realistic use of colloquial language and first-person narrative. Hemingway was hardest hit. When he wasn't bagging big game on Mount Kilimanjaro or reeling in silvery marlin off Cuba, the Lost Generation's centerfold was writing lean and mean tales of stiff upper lips. Today most critics see his macho prose as a macho pose, but we wouldn't throw him out of bed for eating crackers.

"It tolls for thee!"

1920s the dream was picked up by F. Scott Fitzgerald's Jay Gatsby, the tony, buttoned-down Easterner with Huck Finn's irresponsibility; in the 1950s it was time for Huck Lite, in the form of J. D. Salinger's Holden Caulfield.

SLEEPLESS IN CAMELOT

Wacked on the head during a quarrel in a New England munitions factory near Hartford, Hank Morgan awakens in Camelot, King Arthur's sixth-century version of a male-bonding drum rally. Hank is taken to the Round Table, where he is bored by the knights' chest-thumping tales of their chivalry. Overreacting a wee bit to this cold shoulder, Merlin the Magician sentences Hank to burn at the stake. Anxious to avoid the Joan of Arc trick, Hank sends a message that Merlin's a humbug but Hank's the Real Thing. To bolster his claim, Hank says he will destroy the sun if he is killed. Hank knows his history: on June 21, 528, the day of his planned barbecue, there will be a total eclipse of the sun. Sure enough, Hank is lashed to the stake, the sticks are torched, and the sun vanishes. Awed, King Arthur orders Hank released. After solidifying his power with a pyrotechnic display involving dynamite manufactured from scratch, Hank shoulders Merlin aside as resident magician. Merlin, a very sore loser, vows revenge.

Hank and his Yankee ingenuity whip the place into shape, establishing schools, training workers, starting a newspaper, and hooking up the telephones. By the time the Boss is finished, all that's missing is spandex. Challenged to a duel by Sir Sagramour, Hank goes on a quest

WHO'S
HO
☞

A Connecticut Yankee
in King Arthur's Court:
A LITERARY TOUT SHEET

Hank Morgan: Your industrial arts teacher with a brain.

Clarence: The gofer; a page in King Arthur's Court.

King Arthur: Sean Connery without the attitude.

Sandy: Morgan's adoring and adorable wife.

Merlin: Go ahead, make his day.

to get into shape. Along the way he frees Morgan Le Fay's prisoners and repairs a well, embarrassing Merlin once more. Back at Camelot, the Boss wins the duel and makes his day.

Three years pass and the sixth-century backwater has become a thriving nineteenth-century-style metropolis of schools, trains, factories, telephones, and telegraphs. The Boss marries and has a daughter. After a trip to the seashore, he returns to find Camelot in shambles. Arthur has died in a battle with Lancelot over Queen Guinevere, and the Church has destroyed all the Boss's work. In the final battle, Merlin casts a spell over the Boss to make him sleep for thirteen hundred years. As the story ends, the Boss awakens in the nineteenth century.

MISSION IMPOSSIBLE

Hank, like Huck, represents the commonplace person, free from the corruption of hereditary wealth and power. Unlike Huck, however, who is a powerless observer, Hank can "civilize" the world. With the boundless optimism of his age, Twain saw technology as the new social ideal: the greatest product of the greatest society. Hank sees himself as a nineteenth-century Prometheus, freeing the oppressed masses of backward old England. Twain pits his humanitarian values against the selfishness and greed of the aristocracy and the Church, but never stops to examine the ends and the means. It's no wonder that when the smoke clears, the aristocracy has won.

The novel's ending is as bleak as anything Twain ever wrote. In the scenes of Hank's Utopia destroyed by perverse human nature, Twain suggests that there is something innate in people that makes dreams of progress hopeless. The novel anticipates the later Twain, who, after the death of his favorite daughter, the illness of his beloved wife, and his own great financial ruin, became a misanthropic voice crying out against the "damned human race."

AT THE MOVIES

The first movie version of *A Connecticut Yankee* appeared in 1931 and starred Will Rogers as the Boss. Bing Crosby crooned in the 1949 version. It doesn't have any great songs, but it's colorful. A lame MTV version appeared in 1989, the script massacred by teen novelist Paul Zindel as a vehicle for ten-year-old *Cosby* cutie Keshia Knight Pulliam.

SUMMARY

⏱ Elevated truth, justice, and the American way into myth.

⏱ Perfected the paradigm of American humor: the deadpan voice that tells outrageous tales.

⏱ Created an American voice by rendering the rhythms, vocabulary, and tone of American English vernacular.

⏱ Wrote some damned funny stuff.

Stephen Crane, 1871-1900,
American novelist and short story writer, leading
Naturalist

CHAPTER 12

STEPHEN CRANE

(1871–1900)

YOU MUST REMEMBER THIS

Crane as a literary Terminator, attacking tradition through what he said and how he said it. Smashed through nationalism, patriotism, individualism, and organized religion to confront the meaninglessness of the universe.

MOST FAMOUS FOR

Writing *the* great Civil War Book without ever having seen a second of service. Definitely the way to go. His most famous works include:

- ★ *Maggie: A Girl of the Streets* (1893)
- ★ *The Red Badge of Courage: An Episode of the American Civil War* (1895)
- ★ *The Black Riders and Other Lines* (1895) (poetry)
- ★ *War Is Kind* (1899) (poetry)
- ★ "The Open Boat" (1897)

EVEN STEPHEN

Crane had the misfortune of being born in Newark, New Jersey, which meant that his life could only improve. (Please don't send us letters extolling life in Newark. We have been there ourselves.) Papa Crane was devout and Mama Crane fertile: Stephen was the fourteenth child of the Methodist minister and his missus. He attended several schools, including Lafayette College and Syracuse University, but never graduated from anywhere, preferring baseball to books. Among his other talents was a real gift for profanity. When the major leagues and the nineteenth-century version of Andrew Dice Clay didn't come calling, Crane worked as a reporter and wrote freelance articles on the side. And starved.

In 1893 Crane published *Maggie: A Girl of the Streets*. This tale about a good girl who becomes a prostitute because of her environment and heredity left publishers so underwhelmed that Crane scraped together his pennies and published it himself. Next came *Red Badge*, Crane's masterpiece, set during the Civil War. It was a great success and Crane was famous by the time he was twenty-four.

In addition to writing novels, short stories, and poems, Crane traveled to Greece to write newspaper articles about the war with Turkey; shacked up with Cora Howorth Taylor, madam of one of the better whorehouses; and covered the Spanish-American War for William Randolph Hearst. Along the way he became friends with Henry James, Joseph Conrad, and H. G. Wells.

Crane died of malaria and tuberculosis before he was thirty, leaving behind enough quality writing to fill ten fat books. Now don't you feel like a lazy lump?

HART CRANE (1899–1932)

Don't confuse Stephen Crane with fellow writer Hart Crane—the latter had a much more miserable life. Seemingly the most promising poet of his generation, Hart Crane couldn't stop chasing sailors and waiters, chugalugging, and fighting with his parents long enough to finish his wonderful epic poem, *The Bridge*. Crane saw himself as a modern Walt Whitman, a seer and a prophet, but unlike his historical mentor, he was unable to withstand the public's colossal indifference. He could sing, but he couldn't swim, as his suicide off the side of a ship in the Gulf of Mexico tragically proved.

Hart Crane, 1899-1932, the dour American poet unrelated to Stephen Crane.

ISMS

The Mother of Ism: Realism

The Realists, the nineteenth century's answer to Dan Rather and Chuck Scarborough, told it like it was, focusing on the lives of ordinary people, often the denizens of the middle, or lower middle, class. Since the Realists didn't have to contend with sweeps month, they weren't talking schlock about hermaphrodites and the farm animals who love them; instead, they concentrated on pessimistic views of poverty, prostitution, and pain.

Son of Realism: Naturalism

The Naturalists took Realism one step further, from "60 Minutes" to Geraldo and Oprah. Like the Realists, the Naturalists focused on the lives of regular people and attempted to portray life truthfully and accurately. But unlike the Realists, the Naturalists had already worked out the world view: the universe was a nasty place, unpredictable, spontaneous, and discontinuous. A person's fate was determined by environment, heredity, and chance. Free will was an illusion, God a cruel joke. As a result, the Naturalists frequently portrayed characters whose lives were shaped by forces of nature they could neither understand nor control. The advantage of Naturalism is that you never have to read the last page first; you know everyone is going to come to a bad end. The disadvantage? These are not books to read when you're out of Häagen-Dazs and the canary is feet-first in the cage.

Naturalism exploded again in the 1930s in *U.S.A.*, John Dos Passos's panoramic view of America, and *The Grapes of Wrath*, John Steinbeck's readable blockbuster about the Okies. Media darling Norman Mailer looked like the great white hope with his Naturalistic masterpiece *The Naked and the Dead* (1948), but he pooped out somewhere between his sixth marriage and an unsuccessful run for New York City mayor.

LIFE IN HELL

Maggie and her two brothers grow up on the wrong side of the tracks. Both her parents have crawled inside the bottle and set up housekeeping; the children spend a lot of time cowering under the bed as their parents beat each other. One son dies, while the other, Jimmy, follows in his father's footsteps; miraculously, Maggie remains untouched by the filth around her until she falls in love with Jimmy's best friend, the flashy barkeep Pete. Catholic girls start much too late: two dates in the razzle-dazzle Big Apple and Maggie's a Fallen Woman.

But Pete's a fickle fellow, and he soon kicks Maggie out. Her mother and the neighbors, siding with Jimmy in judging Maggie a disgrace, follow suit, and Maggie finds herself out on her rump. Jimmy, an expert in seducing other men's sisters, joins in the general hypocritical indignation and decides to punch out Pete's lights. When Jimmy fails to inflict any real damage, he shrugs his shoulders and lays the blame on Maggie.

Maggie implores Pete to take her back, but he refuses. Homeless and broke, she turns to the world's oldest pro-

WHO'S WHO ☞

Maggie: A Girl of the Streets:
A LITERARY TOUT SHEET

Maggie: The girl next door who becomes a prostitute.

Jimmy: Her alcoholic brother, who has sired enough children to populate a small Latin American country.

Pete: Single white male looking for a good time; photo and phone a must.

The Mother: Mommy Dearest.

fession. But the pickings are slim for the inexperienced and she sinks lower and lower, finally ending up trying to seduce men on the waterfront. Shortly thereafter Jimmy comes home from one of his weeks on the town to find his mother wailing that Maggie has died. The neighbors offer comfort, but Maggie's mother shrieks and laments that she had forgiven her daughter her sins.

WORKING NINE TO FIVE

The publication of *Maggie* in 1893, when Crane was only twenty-two, heralded a major new talent in American literature. The first novel to deal realistically with the sordid life of the slums, *Maggie* has been called the first truly modern American novel, the first Naturalistic novel, and the first novel that divides the English novel from the American. It was also the first novel to deal sympathetically with s-e-x and with the Fallen Woman. Crane's attack on the hypocritical religious values of the late nineteenth century opened the floodgates for the loss of traditional values, a major twentieth-century theme. Alcoholism, child abuse, and run-ins with the law were okay—but sex? Saints preserve us! Whatever else it did, *Maggie* separated the writers from the wusses and announced that Crane was a major literary talent.

The novel traces how people are controlled by their environment and heredity: Maggie never stood a snowball's chance in heck. Crane's inscription to a friend read: "For it [the novel] tries to show that environment is a tremendous thing in the world and frequently shapes lives regardless." In this sense, the novel is as much about the environment as it is about Maggie.

THEODORE DREISER (1871–1945)

Dreiser made it to the short list for the Nobel Prize, but Sinclair Lewis copped the gold instead. A shining light in the Naturalist heaven, Dreiser had the advantage of a long life and a miserable childhood. He is best known for his wretched style and massive novels, which double as doorstops. *Sister Carrie*, a heavily blue-penciled story about a Fallen Woman, was issued in 1900; the uncensored version did not come out until the 1980s. Dreiser's blockbusters include *An American Tragedy* (1925) and his "trilogy of desire": *The Financier* (1912), *The Titan* (1914), and *The Stoic* (1947), published posthumously. Aside from being a Naturalist's Naturalist, he was one of the first to state the twentieth-century golden rule: Those with the gold rule.

So What Did *You* Do in the War, Daddy?

Chapter 1

The cold passed reluctantly from the earth, and the retiring fogs revealed an army stretched out on the hills, resting. As the landscape changed from brown to green, the army awakened, and it began to tremble with eagerness at the noise of rumors. It cast its eyes upon the roads, which were growing from long troughs of liquid mud to proper thoroughfares. A river, amber-tinted in the shadows of its banks, purled at the army's feet; and at night, when the stream had become of a sorrowful blackness, one could see across it the red, eyelike gleam of hostile camp-fires set in the low brows of distant hills.

Sound-bite summary: Young member of the Union Army panics when he faces battle for the first time but recovers from his fright as the story progresses.

Novel-for-television summary: Dripping wet behind the ears, Henry Fleming listens to the tall soldier, Jim Conklin, and the loud soldier, Wilson, argue over the rumor that the troops are about to move. A farm boy, Henry is just itching to see action. The troops do indeed move, but it is only to make another march. When the fighting finally begins, Henry starts off at ground zero, lost in the haze. Suddenly, he finds himself in the middle of the attack, firing his rifle over and over. The skirmish ends as suddenly as it had begun, and Henry is astonished to see the sun shining blue over all the carnage. In the middle of the mop-up, the enemy springs another attack. Exhausted and unprepared, the men beat a hasty retreat. Henry joins the pack.

In an orgy of guilt, Henry hightails it to the forest but later rejoins his fellows and realizes that he is the only one without a war wound, a "red badge of courage." Henry approaches a badly injured soldier, horrified to find that it is Jim Conklin. Despite Henry's help, Jim dies. Henry heads for the hills once again.

Henry envies the dead; they are already heroes and he is a coward. As he nears his regiment, the men break ranks and run frantically in his direction, shouting incoherently. One man hits him with his rifle butt: Henry sees stars. He walks a long while until he makes his way back to his regiment. There, he speaks with Wilson, who had been a blowhard before the battle. Henry now feels superior and manages to forget his cowardice.

WHO'S
H
O
☞

> # *The Red Badge of Courage:*
> ## A LITERARY TOUT SHEET
>
> **Henry Fleming:** The callow youth who Finds Himself.
>
> **Jim Conklin:** The tall soldier.
>
> **Wilson:** The loud soldier.
>
> **The Tattered Soldier:** The soldier who reflects Henry's early infatuation with the blood and guts of war.
>
> **Mrs. Fleming:** Henry's mother, the simple, uneducated farm woman who has a brief guest shot.

Anther battle starts, and this time Henry takes it on the chin. Everyone praises him as a hero; Henry knows that he behaved like a lunatic. At the next battle, Henry gets to hold the flag. When the smoke clears, he feels that he can judge his own courage.

YOU'RE IN THE ARMY NOW

Crane never intended *The Red Badge of Courage* to be a history of the Civil War, so ignore that subtitle. Instead, he was going the Stephen King route minus the horror— a psychological portrayal of fear. As seen through the eyes of "the youth," Henry Fleming, the novel becomes cosmic in scope because it deals with some of the major reasons we pop Valium like Tic-Tacs: isolation, lack of identity, failure, guilt, fear of death. Henry finds his identity, learns that courage is unselfishness, and is able to judge himself dispassionately. In short, he finally joins the major leagues.

The book that established Crane as one of the literary movers and shakers is considered the first truly modern war novel. Ironically, when he wrote the book Crane had never seen a war, much less fought in one: wars can be tough to find, and the Civil War was six years in the past when he was born. But he had done his homework, and his portrait of the war was so vivid that several early reviewers were adamant that only a war-scarred battle veteran could have written the book. Which shows you what reviewers know.

HISTORY LESSONS

For you history buffs, Chancellorsville is the battle described in the novel; the generals were Joseph Hooker (Union) and Robert E. Lee and Stonewall Jackson (Confederate). Nearly thirty thousand men perished in the encounter, including Stonewall himself, mistakenly shot in the darkness by one of his own men. None of this is mentioned in the novel.

Thomas Jonathan ("Stonewall") Jackson, 1824-1863, famous American Confederate general

While Henry is often propelled by outside actions, he is no mere flotsam on the river of life—the case with the characters of most Naturalistic novels. Henry loses his identity as part of the war machine, but he is capable of independent action; for example, he consciously chooses to hit the road during the first battle. The novel is also admired for its memorable imagery, such as guns that "belched and howled like brass dev-

Civil War carnage

ils guarding the gate" or "squatted in a row like savage chiefs." His use of color is especially vivid—"red eyes," "blue demonstration," "red sun." The writing does get a little arty, but hey, the kid was twenty-four when he wrote it.

THE OPEN BOAT
A TALE INTENDED TO BE AFTER THE FACT, BEING THE EXPERIENCE OF FOUR MEN FROM THE SUNK STEAMER COMMODORE

None of them knew the color of the sky. Their eyes glanced level, and were fastened upon the waves that swept toward them. These waves were of the hue of slate, save for the tops, which were of foaming white, and all of the men knew the colors of the sea. The horizon narrowed and widened, and dipped and rose, and at all times its edge was jagged with waves that seemed thrust up in points like rocks.

Many a man ought to have a bath-tub larger than the boat which here rode upon the sea. These waves were most wrongfully and barbarously abrupt and tall, and each froth-top was a problem in small boat navigation. . . .

As dawn breaks, the four men adrift in the small dinghy off the Florida coast begin to realize that they *have* been in better situations. The oiler and correspondent are rowing in an attempt to reach the lifesaving station that the cook claims is located at Mosquito Inlet Light. Spirits sink, but the captain, although badly injured, jollies the men along. After a long while the men spy a lighthouse far on the horizon and fashion a sail from the captain's coat. The beach is deserted, but the men do not realize that the cook knows his poached pears better than his geography—there is no lifesaving station. The men row on, despite their aching muscles.

Suddenly, they spot a man on the beach. They scream to attract his attention, and an omnibus from one of the large resorts drives onto the sand. Since the people on the beach are part of an outing, not a rescue party, they assume that the men in the boat are bored fishermen and ignore them. The wind shifts, the sun sets, and the men are adrift on the indifferent sea.

The exhausted men sleep as best they can, despite the crashing waves that drench them with icy blasts. The oiler, the strongest of the lot, does most of the rowing. Finally, even he falls asleep and the correspondent rows all alone. For company, he has an enormous shark trolling for a midnight snack. As is the tendency of people sitting up late at night in a small boat on the open sea, the correspondent muses on his fate:

"If I am going to be drowned—if I am going to be drowned—if I am going to be drowned, why, in the name of the seven mad gods who rule the sea, was I allowed to come thus far and contemplate sand and trees? Was I brought here merely to have my nose dragged away as I was about to nibble the sacred cheese of life? It is preposterous. If this old ninny-woman, Fate, cannot do better than this, she should be deprived of the management of men's fortunes. She is an old hen who knows not her intention. If she has decided to drown me, why did she not do it in the beginning and save me all this trouble. The whole affair is absurd. . . ."

Finally, the shark heads for the ocean equivalent of 7-Eleven, the oiler awakens and relieves him, and the correspondent sleeps.

The next morning the desperate men realize that they have to get the boat to shore very soon or die. The treacherous surf makes it highly unlikely that they will survive. As they approach shore, the men jump into the raging sea. The oiler, and the correspondent, a wimp but desperate for a happy ending, swim for it. The injured captain and cook cling to the capsized boat. Ironically, the only one to perish is the oiler, seemingly the strongest of the lot.

WHO'S WHO ☞

"The Open Boat":
A LITERARY TOUT SHEET

The Correspondent: Crane recalls a very sticky situation.

The Oiler ("Billy"): Rocky Balboa of the seafaring set.

The Cook: If I only had a heart; the cowardly lion of the crowd.

The Captain: The old salt, brave and bluff.

The Sea: We eat our young; as heartless as disgruntled Mets' fans.

CRUISE TO NOWHERE

On January 1, 1897, Crane sailed to Cuba on the *Commodore* to report on the Spanish-American War. He should have taken Greyhound: early the following morning, the *Commodore* sank like a stone. He and three other men spent nearly thirty terrifying hours in a ten-foot dinghy before landing at Daytona, Florida. But the story is more than a lesson in listening to your English teacher screaming, "Write about what you know, dummy."

The story concerns the conflict between humanity and nature. The sea, a symbol for nature, is indifferent to people. Alternately cruel and kind, teasing or menacing, the sea is as heartless as acne. Survival on the sea is a matter of total chance. Humanity's struggles are grimly ironic: the oiler, the strongest of the group, drowns, but the wounded captain and cowardly cook survive. Crane and the Careful Reader realize the accident of their existence, the tenuousness of life.

"The Open Boat" has become the poster child for Naturalism because of Crane's use of imagery to portray nature's heartless indifference. The boat is compared to a "bath-tub"; the waves are "slate walls" and have "snarling" crests. The correspondent thinks of himself as a mouse, a puny creature incapable of doing more than "nibble the sacred cheese of life." The famous line "None of them knew the color of the sky" emphasizes the single-minded focus on survival, on glimpsing the land over the jagged horizon. Further, Crane does not name the men—they are the "correspondent," "cook," and "captain"—to show that they are as anonymous as pieces of driftwood. Ironically, the only character with a name, the oiler Billy, perishes, as though having an identity marks a person for death.

From *War Is Kind*

9 6

A man said to the universe:
"Sir, I exist!"
"However," replied the universe,
"The fact has not created in me
A sense of obligation."

THE SPANISH-AMERICAN WAR

The Spanish-American War was newspaper mogul William Randolph Hearst's 1898 do-it-yourself war, and a neat job it was, too. Ostensibly, the United States waged the war against Spain to liberate Cuba from Spanish rule; in reality, before the days of NutraSweet, people consumed a lot of Cuban sugar. The actual war was as brief as a Liz Taylor marriage: hostilities began on April 24; the peace treaty was signed on December 10. As a result of the nastiness, the United States became a world power.

Colonel Summer's command advancing to the
Battle of Moasin, American Civil War

From *Posthumously Published Poems*

113

A man adrift on a slim spar
A horizon smaller than the rim of a bottle
Tented waves rearing lashy dark points
The near whine of froth in circles.
        God is cold.

The incessant raise and swing of the sea
And growl after growl of crest
The sinkings, green, seething, endless
The upheaval half-completed,
        God is cold.

THE BEAVER IS NOT HAPPY

Crane's poetry, like his fiction and his life, is a slash-and-burn attack on everything the nineteenth century cherished: God, nature, love, justice, and the glory of war. Along the way he rejects rhyme and traditional rhythms. The major theme, the same as in his prose, is humanity's utter inability to perceive truth and our amazing willingness to believe that we do indeed see it. For Crane, the world is chaotic, and all humanity's beliefs about God and nations, religion, and history are entirely delusory. Ultimately, his poetry is a protest against life and the lies that we tell ourselves to make it all tolerable.

SUMMARY

⏱ Did for Naturalism what Fort Lauderdale did for Spring Break.

⏱ Threw out conventional plot to embrace the mental life of his characters.

⏱ Cultivated a brilliant, innovative, ironic style, chock-full of images and metaphors.

⏱ Employed penetrating psychological realism.

abolitionism, 53, 119, 121, 122, 125
    Douglass and, 117–28
    Garrison and, 119, 124–25, 127
    Truth and, 122
Adventures of Huckleberry Finn, The
    (Twain), xiii, 193, 201–6
Adventures of Tom Sawyer, The
    (Twain), 193, 201
African-American literature, 126
    slave narratives, 125–27
Alcott, Bronson, 42, 134
Alhambra, The (Irving), 3, 6
Allan, Frances, 80
Allan, John, 80, 81
allegory, 184
Allen, Woody, 195, 201
"American Scholar, The" (Emer-
    son), 48–49
American Tragedy, An (Dreiser), 219
Anderson, Sherwood, 206
"Annabel Lee" (Poe), 79, 87
Anthony, Susan B., 121
Autocrat of the Breakfast Table, The
    (Holmes), 49

Bailey, Harriet, 118
Baldwin, James, 126
"Bartleby, the Scrivener" (Melville),
    165–68
baseball, 23
Baudelaire, Charles, 82, 83, 95
Beecher, Catherine, 100
Beecher, Lyman, 100
Benét, Stephen Vincent, 16, 199
Biggers, Earl Deer, 96
Billy Budd (Melville), 151, 162–65
black literature, 126
    slave narratives, 125–27
Blithedale Romance, The (Hawthorne),
    59, 62, 72–76
bowling, 11, 12
Bracebridge Hall (Irving), 3, 6
Brackenridge, Hugh Henry, 26
Bradbury, Ray, 144
Bradstreet, Anne, 179
Bride of Lammermoor, The (Scott), 120
Bridge, The (Crane), 215
Brook Farm, 42, 74, 75
Brooklyn Eagle, 132, 153
Brooks, Gwendolyn, 126
Brown, Charles Brockden, 26

Brown, John, 52, 53, 122
Browne, Charles Farrar, 195
Bryant, William Cullen, 7, 8
Bunyan, John, 184
Burr, Aaron, 4, 5
Bush, Trevor, 56
Byron, Anne Isabella, Lady, 103
Byron, George Gordon, Lord, xi,
    103, 120

"Calamus" poems (Whitman), 139,
    147
Carroll, Lewis, 195
Castle of Otranto, The (Walpole), 91
catalog technique, 139
"Celebrated Jumping Frog of Cala-
    veras County, The" (Twain),
    193, 197–201
"Chambered Nautilus, The"
    (Holmes), 49
Champion of Virtue, The (Reeve), 91
Chancellorsville, 222
Chandler, Raymond, 96
Channing, William Ellery, 42, 74
Chesnutt, Charles W., 126
Chesterton, G. K., 96
Christie, Agatha, 96
"Civil Disobedience" (Thoreau), 41,
    55–57
Civil War, xiii, 99, 122
    Red Badge of Courage and, 213,
        214, 219–24
    Whitman and, 134, 142
    see also slavery
Coleridge, Samuel Taylor, 52
colloquial and vernacular language,
    xiii, 201, 206, 211
Confidence Man, The (Melville), 44
*Connecticut Yankee in King Arthur's
    Court, A* (Twain), 193, 207–9
    film versions of, 210
Conrad, Joseph, 37, 214
Cooper, James Fenimore, x–xi,
    21–39, 68, 206
    The Deerslayer, 21, 27, 31–35
    The Last of the Mohicans, xi, 21,
        27, 28–31
    The Leatherstocking Tales, 21, 27–37
    The Pilot, 21, 25, 35, 37
Cooper, Susan DeLancey, 24–25
Cooperstown, 22, 23

Covey, Edward, 119
Crane, Hart, 215
Crane, Stephen, xiii–xiv, 213–30
　Maggie: A Girl of the Streets, xiv,
　　213, 214, 216–18
　"The Open Boat," 213, 224–28
　poetry of, 213, 228, 229
　The Red Badge of Courage, 213,
　　214, 219–24
"Crossing Brooklyn Ferry" (Whit-
　man), 135–36
Crucible, The (Miller), 61

Damn Yankees, 16
Dana, Charles Ellery, 74
death, as theme, xii, 183–85, 188–90
Deerslayer, The (Cooper), 21, 27,
　31–35
detective stories, xi, 79, 94, 95, 96,
　97
devil, souls sold to, 16
"Devil and Daniel Webster, The"
　(Benét), 16, 199
"Devil and Tom Walker, The" (Ir-
　ving), 16–18
Dickens, Charles, 7, 195
Dickinson, Emily, xii, 44, 173–91
Doktor Faustus (Mann), 16
Doolittle, Hilda (H. D.), 177
Dos Passos, John, 216
Doubleday, Abner, 23
Douglass, Anna Murray, 120
Douglass, Charles, 122
Douglass, Frederick, xiii, 117–29
　name change of, 118, 120
　newspaper of, 121, 127
Douglass, Lewis, 122
Doyle, Arthur Conan, 94, 95, 96
Dreiser, Theodore, 44, 95, 219
Dr. Faustus (Marlowe), 16
Du Bois, W. E. B., 126
Dunbar, Paul Laurence, 126

Eliot, George, 195
Eliot, T. S., 94
Ellison, Ralph, 126
Emerson, Ellen Tucker, 45
Emerson, Ralph Waldo, xi, 41, 42,
　44–52, 56, 68, 188
　Essays, 41, 46–50
　poetry of, xi, 50–51
　quotes from, 47
　Whitman and, 133, 139
epics, 160, 161

Equiano, Olaudah, 125
Essays (Emerson), 41, 46–50

Fanshawe (Hawthorne), 60
Faulkner, William, 77, 95–96, 206
Faust (Goethe), 16
feminism, 121
Financier, The (Dreiser), 219
Fireside Poets, 134
Fitzgerald, F. Scott, 146, 207
Fleurs de mal, Les (Baudelaire), 83
Forster, E. M., 144
Frankenstein (Shelley), 91
Frederick Douglass' Paper (The North
　Star), 121, 127
free verse, xii, 136–37, 149, 184
Frost, Robert, 44, 137
Fuller, Margaret, 42, 43

Gandhi, Mahatma, 56
Gansevoort, Guert, 164–65
Gardner, Erle Stanley, 96
Garrison, William Lloyd, 119,
　124–25, 127
Goethe, Johann Wolfgang von, 16
"Gold Bug, The" (Poe), 79, 92–94
Golden Bowl (James), 35
Golding, William, 189
Good Gray Poet, The (Whitman), 132
Gothic literature, 91, 184
Grapes of Wrath, The (Steinbeck), 216
Griswold, Rufus, 82

Hamilton, Alexander, 5
Hammett, Dashiell, 96
Hammond, Jupiter, 126
Harrison, William Henry, 123
Hathorne, John, 60
Hathorne, William, 60
Hawthorne, Nathaniel, xii, 7, 59–77,
　90, 154, 188
　The Blithedale Romance, 59, 62,
　　72–76
　The House of the Seven Gables, 59,
　　62, 68–72, 75
　The Scarlet Letter, xii, 35, 59,
　　62–68, 75
Hawthorne, Sophia Peabody, 60–62
Hayes, Rutherford B., 122
Hearst, William Randolph, 214, 228
Hemingway, Ernest, 193, 206
Henry, O., 195
Higginson, Thomas Wentworth, 177
History of New York from the Beginning
　of the World to the End of the
　Dutch Dynasty (Irving), 3, 4–5

History of the Life and Voyages of Co-
lumbus (Irving), 6
Holmes, Oliver Wendell, Jr., 49
Holmes, Oliver Wendell, Sr., 48, 49,
134
Holmes, Sherlock, 95
Homer, 139
Hooker, Joseph, 222
Hoover, J. Edgar, 126
House of the Seven Gables, The (Haw-
thorne), 59, 62, 68–72, 75
Hughes, Langston, 126
humor, 201, 211
Hurston, Zora Neale, 126
"Hymn Sung at the Completion of
the Concord Monument, April
19, 1836" (Emerson), 50–51

imagism, 177
"In a Station of the Metro"
(Pound), 177
Innocents Abroad, The (Twain), 193,
196
*Interesting Narrative of the Life of Olau-
dah Equiano, or Gustavus Vassa,
the African* (Equiano), 125
Iroquois, 30, 31, 33, 34
Irving, Washington, x–xi, 3–19, 26,
68
    "The Devil and Tom Walker,"
    16–18
    "The Legend of Sleepy Hollow,"
    xi, 3, 6, 7–10
    "The Legend of the Moor's Leg-
    acy," 13–15
    pseudonyms of, 3
    "Rip Van Winkle," 3, 6, 10–13
Irving, William, 4
"I Sing the Body Electric" (Brad-
bury), 144
"I Sing the Body Electric" (Whitman), 137–39

Jackson, Stonewall, 222
James, Henry, 35, 60, 67, 94, 214
Jefferson, Thomas, 4, 24
Jewett, Sarah Orne, 113
John Dollar (Wiggins), 189

Keats, John, 52
King, Martin Luther, Jr., 56

"Lady of the Lake, The" (Scott),
120
Lardner, Ring, 146

Last of the Mohicans, The (Cooper),
xi, 21, 27, 28–31
    film versions of, 30
Lawrence, D. H., 22
Leatherstocking Tales, The (Cooper),
21, 27–37
Leaves of Grass (Whitman), ix, xii,
131, 133–34, 138
    "Calamus" section of, 139, 147
Lee, Robert E., 53, 222
"Legend of Sleepy Hollow, The"
(Irving), xi, 3, 6, 7–10
"Legend of the Moor's Legacy,
The" (Irving), 13–15
"Lenore" (Poe), 79, 88
Letter to His Countrymen, A (Cooper),
21, 26
Lewis, Sinclair, 219
*Life and Times of Frederick Douglass,
The* (Douglass), 117, 127–28
Life on the Mississippi (Twain), 193,
196
"Ligeia" (Poe), 79, 88–91
Lincoln, Abraham, xiii, 99
    Whitman's elegy for, 141–43
"Lines Composed a Few Miles
Above Tintern Abbey" (Words-
worth), 145
Longfellow, Henry Wadsworth, 7,
134, 145
Long Island, 132, 145, 146
Lord, Otis P., 180
Lord of the Flies (Golding), 189
Lowell, Amy, 177
Lowell, James Russell, 134

McCarthy, Joe, 57, 61
Maggie: A Girl of the Streets (Crane),
xiv, 213, 214, 216–18
Mailer, Norman, 216
Mallarmé, Stéphane, 95
Mann, Thomas, 16
Mardi (Melville), 151, 153, 154
Marlowe, Christopher, 16
Masters, Edgar Lee, 113, 114
Melvill, Allan, 152
Melvill, Maria Gansevoort, 152, 155
Melville, Elizabeth Shaw, 153
Melville, Frances, 155
Melville, Herman, xii, 37, 44, 68, 77,
127, 151–71, 188
    "Bartleby, the Scrivener," 165–68
    Billy Budd, 151, 162–65
    Irving and, 7
Moby Dick, xii, 151, 154, 155–61, 171

metaphor, 184
meter, 136, 184
Miller, Arthur, 61
Milton, John, 139
"Moby Dick," 160
Moby Dick (Melville), xii, 151, 154, 155–61, 171
Morrison, Toni, 126
Mott, Lucretia, 121
My Bondage and My Freedom (Douglass), 117, 127
"My Lost Youth" (Longfellow), 145
Mysteries of Udolpho, The (Radcliffe), 91

Naked and the Dead, The (Mailer), 216
Narrative of the Life of Frederick Douglass, an American Slave (Douglass), xiii, 117, 123–27
National Baseball Hall of Fame and Museum, 23
Native Americans, xi, 30, 31, 33, 34, 35–36, 194
Naturalism, xiii–xiv, 216, 218, 219, 223, 227, 230
Nature (Emerson), 41, 45, 46–48
nervous disorders, in women, 175
New York Stock Exchange, 166
"Noiseless Patient Spider, A" (Whitman), 140–41
Norris, Frank, 95
North Star, 121, 127

"Old Ironsides" (Holmes), 49
Oldtown Folks (Stowe), 99, 110–14
Omoo (Melville), 151, 153
"Open Boat, The" (Crane, 213, 224–28
Orwell, George, 195
"Out of the Cradle, Endlessly Rocking" (Whitman), 144–46

Paradis artificiels, Les (Baudelaire), 83
Parker, Theodore, 42, 74
Passage to India (Forster), 144
"Passage to India" (Whitman), 143–44
Pathfinder, The (Cooper), 21, 27
pen names, 195
of Irving, 3
Perelman, S. J., 201
personification, 184

"Philosophy of Composition, The" (Poe), 86
Pierce, Franklin, 62
Pierre (Melville), 151, 154
Pilgrim's Progress (Bunyan), 184
Pilot, The (Cooper), 21, 25, 36, 37
Pioneers, The (Cooper), 21, 25, 27
"Plea for Captain John Brown" (Thoreau), 52
Poe, Edgar Allan, xi, 68, 79–97
"The Gold Bug," 79, 92–94
"Ligeia," 79, 88–91
poetry of, xi, 79, 80, 82, 84–88
Poe, Virginia, 81, 82
poetry:
catalog technique in, 139
of Crane, 213, 228, 229
of Dickinson, xii, 173–91
of Emerson, xi, 50–51
free verse, xii, 136–37, 149, 184
imagist, 177
meter in, 136, 184
of Poe, xi, 79, 80, 82, 84–88
rhyme in, 134, 136, 177, 184
rhythm in, 134, 136, 177, 184
sonnets, 134
of Whitman, xii, 131–49, 184
Posthumously Published Poems (Crane), 229
Pound, Ezra, 177
Prairie, The (Cooper), 21, 27, 37
Precaution (Cooper), 25
pseudonyms, 195
of Irving, 3
Puritans, xii, 63, 64, 67, 68, 75

Radcliffe, Ann, 91
"Raven, The" (Poe), 79, 82, 84–86
Realism, 215, 216, 218, 230
Naturalism, xiii–xiv, 216, 218, 219, 223, 227, 230
Red Badge of Courage, The: An Episode of the American Civil War (Crane), xiv, 213, 214, 219–24
Redburn (Melville), 151, 153
Reeve, Clara, 91
rhyme, 134, 136, 177, 184
rhythm, 134, 136, 177, 184
Ripley, George, 74
"Rip Van Winkle" (Irving), 3, 6, 10–13
"Rip Van Winkle's Lilacs" (Melville), 7
Robinson, Edwin Arlington, 95
Rob Roy (Scott), 120

Romanticism, x–xi, 52, 68, 145, 187
Rossetti, Dante Gabriel, 95
Rushdie, Salman, 189

Salinger, J. D., 207
Salmagundi, 4
Sayers, Dorothy, 96
Scarlet Letter, The (Hawthorne), xii, 35, 59, 62–68, 75
"Scented Herbage of My Breast" (Whitman), 146–47
Scott, Sir Walter, 7, 25, 120
"Self-Reliance" (Emerson), 49–50
Shakespeare, William, 134
Shaw, George Bernard, 95
Shelley, Mary Wollstonecraft, 91
Shelley, Percy Bysshe, xi, 52
short story, xi, 79, 90, 97
simile, 184
Sister Carrie (Dreiser), 219
Sketch Book, The (Irving), 3, 6, 7
slave narratives, 125–27
slavery, 52, 53, 100, 101, 102
    Adventures of Huckleberry Finn and, xiii, 205
    Douglass and, xiii, 117–28
    Truth and, 122
    Uncle Tom's Cabin and, xiii, 99, 102, 103–9
    Underground Railroad and, 107, 119
    see also abolitionism
"Song of Myself" (Whitman), xii, 132
sonnets, 134
Spanish-American War, 228
Spoon River Anthology (Masters), 113, 114
Spy, The (Cooper), 21, 25
Stanton, Elizabeth Cady, 121
Steinbeck, John, 216
Stevens, Wallace, 44
Stevenson, Robert Louis, 95
Stoic, The (Dreiser), 219
Stout, Rex, 96
Stowe, Calvin, 100–101
Stowe, Harriet Beecher, 99–115
    Oldtown Folks, 99, 110–14
    Uncle Tom's Cabin, xiii, 99, 102, 103–9, 113
suffragettes, 121

Tales of a Traveller (Irving), 3, 6, 17
tall tales, 200, 201
Tamerlane and Other Poems (Poe), 80

Taylor, Cora Howorth, 214
Taylor, Edward, 179
temperance movement, 121
"Thanatopsis" (Bryant), 8
Thoreau, Henry David, xi, 41, 42, 44, 46, 51–57, 68, 134, 175, 188
    "Civil Disobedience," 41, 55–57
    quotes from, 47
    Walden, 41, 51, 53–55, 57
Thurber, James, 201
Titan, The (Dreiser), 219
Todd, Mabel Loomis, 177, 178
Transcendentalism, xi–xiii, 41–44, 74, 144
    Romanticism and, 52
    Unitarianism and, 45
    see also Emerson, Ralph Waldo; Thoreau, Henry David
Truth, Sojourner, 122
Twain, Mark, 7, 193–211
    The Adventures of Huckleberry Finn, xiii, 193, 201–6
    "The Celebrated Jumping Frog of Calaveras County," 193, 197–201
    A Connecticut Yankee in King Arthur's Court, 193, 207–9, 210
Twain, Olivia Langdon, 196
Twice-Told Tales (Hawthorne), 59, 60, 90
Tyler, John, 81
Typee (Melville), 151, 153, 168–70

Uncle Tom's Cabin (Stowe), xiii, 99, 102, 103–9, 113
    film and play version of, 105, 109
Underground Railroad, 107, 119
Unitarianism, 44, 45
Up from Slavery: An Autobiography (Washington), 125
U.S.A. (Dos Passos), 216

vernacular and colloquial language, xiii, 201, 206, 211
Voltaire, 195

Wadsworth, Charles, 174, 179–80
Walden, or, Life in the Woods (Thoreau), xi, 41, 51, 53–55, 57
Walker, Alice, 126
Walpole, Horance, 91
War Is Kind (Crane), 213, 228
Washington, Booker T., 125
Waverly (Scott), 120
Webster, Daniel, 199

Week on the Concord and Merrimack Rivers, A (Thoreau), 41, 51
Weir, S. Mitchell, 175
Wells, H. G., 214
whaling, 158, 161
Wheatley, Phillis, 126
"When Lilacs last in the Dooryard Bloom'd" (Whitman), 141–43
White, E. B., 55
White Jacket (Melville), 151, 153
Whitman, Walt, ix, xii, 127, 131–49, 215
  Emerson and, 44, 551
  free verse invented by, xii, 136–37, 149, 184
  Melville and, 153
Whittier, John Greenleaf, 134
Wiggins, Marianne, 189
Williams, William Carlos, 177
witchcraft, 61
women, "nervous disorders" in, 175
women's rights, 121
Wordsworth, William, 52, 145
Wright, Richard, 126

ABOUT THE AUTHOR

LAURIE ROZAKIS, Ph.D., is an associate professor of English and Humanities at the State University of New York. Dr. Rozakis is the recipient of a number of awards, including a 1994 Chancellor's Award for Excellence in Teaching, inclusion in the authoritative reference text *Something About the Author*, and several Empire State Challenge Fellowships. Dr. Rozakis' scholarly writing includes entries in *The Dictionary of American Biography*, *Merriam-Webster's Guide to Parliamentary Procedure*, books on young adult authors, and articles on Hawthorne and the other Transcendental writers. She has written for Prentice Hall Literature, Scholastic, Macmillan, Random House, Simon and Schuster, Glenco/McGraw Hill, IBM, Steck-Vaughn, and McDougal, Littell. Dr. Rozakis lives on Long Island with her husband and two children.